SHRM CP/SCP Exam Prep

Mastering HR Concepts with Tips and Strategies for Easy Certification Success | Questions and Detailed Answers Included

Albert Mallin

Introduction

Overview of SHRM CP/SCP Exam

The Society for Human Resource Management Certified Professional (SHRM CP) and Senior Certified Professional (SHRM SCP) exams are prestigious qualifications recognized globally. They validate the competency of HR professionals in applying key HR knowledge and skills in daily operations and strategic decision-making.

The SHRM CP and SCP exams aim to bridge the gap between learning and practical application of knowledge in varied HR situations. They are designed for HR professionals looking to enhance their credibility, improve career opportunities, and broaden their knowledge and skills within the profession.

The SHRM CP exam is designed for HR professionals engaged in operational roles. These individuals focus on HR program implementation, serve as a point of contact for staff and stakeholders, deliver HR services, and perform operational HR functions. On the other hand, the SHRM SCP exam is for those in strategic roles. These professionals develop strategies, lead the HR function, foster influence in the community, analyze performance metrics, and align HR strategies with organizational goals.

Each exam is based on the SHRM Body of Competency and Knowledge (BoCK), which consists of two main areas: the Behavioral Competency Cluster and the Technical Competency Domain. The behavioral cluster focuses on leadership, interpersonal, and business skills, while the technical domain covers areas like people, organization, workplace, and strategy.

The SHRM-CP and SHRM-SCP exams consist of 160 questions each, out of which 95 are knowledge items, and 65 are situational judgment items. The exam's duration is four hours, and the questions are multiple-choice. Knowledge items test the candidate's understanding of factual information, while situational judgment items assess the ability to make decisions in various HR situations.

Both exams are administered by computer in test centers worldwide. They are offered twice a year, during a spring window (May - July) and a winter window (December - February). The specific dates vary each year.

The SHRM CP and SCP exams are scored on a scale of 120 to 200, and a passing score varies with each exam administration due to SHRM's use of the Modified Angoff method to set the cut score. Test-takers will receive preliminary pass/fail notifications immediately after completing the exam, with official results sent by mail approximately four weeks later.

Understanding the structure and requirements of the SHRM CP and SCP exams is the first step towards a successful exam preparation journey. These certifications are not just another feather in your cap; they are a testament to your commitment to the HR profession and your resolve to stay updated with the latest industry trends. They demonstrate your ability to apply HR principles effectively in real-world situations, making you a valuable asset to any organization.

Importance of Certification

Earning your SHRM-CP or SHRM-SCP credential places you in an elite group of HR professionals who have proven their focus, knowledge, and competency in the field. Less than 30% of HR practitioners hold this certification, so being able to add those coveted letters after your name immediately boosts your resume and career potential. This chapter will explore why SHRM certification makes a difference for both individual HR careers and organizational success.

Becoming SHRM certified validates your expertise in key areas that are highly valued by employers. The rigorous exam tests your competencies across HR knowledge domains like people, organization, workforce and strategy. Passing demonstrates that you have mastered critical concepts needed to perform HR jobs at a high level and align to SHRM's behavioral standards model. This knowledge credibility gives you an advantage when interviewing or looking to advance.

The certification process also shows your dedication to the profession. Preparing for the exam requires a real investment of time and effort in studying, practicing, and committing HR theories to memory. For some, it may require months of preparation across more than a dozen textbooks and training programs. Not everyone is willing to make this commitment, and your determination to earn certification displays your motivation to grow and develop as an HR practitioner.

Beyond individual benefits, organizations seek out SHRM-certified professionals for good reason. Research shows that employing more certified HR staff leads to better business outcomes and higher financial performance. Companies with more SHRM-CP's and SCP's tend to see increased employee retention, engagement, and productivity. This results from certified staff developing people-first, strategically-aligned HR policies that support the organization's objectives. Credibility with executives also improves.

There are specific advantages to hiring SHRM-certified professionals versus those holding other credentials like PHR or SPHR. The regular SHRM exam updates ensure certified individuals are current on the latest HR laws, trends, and best practices. The behavioral standards focus assesses judgment, critical thinking, and leadership potential – key qualities when hiring. And SHRM's brand recognition provides hiring credibility.

For consulting firms and HR vendors, employing more SHRM-certified consultants provides a competitive edge in marketing services and lends expertise credibility. Clients are more likely to trust firms with many SHRM-CP's and SCP's on staff to provide data-based, ethical, risk-mitigating guidance. Individuals benefit from improved project opportunities and authority.

Within your organization, becoming SHRM certified can position you for leadership roles. It signals your commitment to the field while validating your strategic business orientation. Certification also keeps you accountable to upholding high professional ethics standards – an important consideration for positions of authority. Mentoring other staff to earn their SHRM credentials further builds your personal leadership brand.

There are also financial incentives associated with certification. A number of studies reveal that SHRM-CP and SCP holders tend to earn higher salaries than their non-certified colleagues, often by a significant margin. One survey showed a 12% average pay boost just for having the credential. Entry level positions may see smaller gains, but the potential earnings upside is substantial over your career, easily offsetting exam costs.

Beyond pay, many organizations provide tuition reimbursement, exam fee coverage, bonuses, and other perks to employees who earn SHRM certification. Taking advantage of these incentives provides you a positive ROI while showcasing your development initiative to leadership. Some companies even mandate SHRM certification for all HR staff – a trend that seems likely to continue. Getting certified proactively future-proofs your job.

The opportunities for professional development available through SHRM membership after certification also add value. From local chapter events, to online webinars, to discounted conferences, there are abundant options to continue expanding your HR skills after the exam. Earning certification is just the first step in a lifelong learning journey.

In summary, the SHRM-CP and SHRM-SCP credentials deliver manifold benefits for your career advancement, leadership potential, financial earnings, professional credibility, and beyond. The quantifiable value proposition combined with intangible benefits make certification extremely worthwhile. When you leverage SHRM credentials strategically within your organization and career, the possibilities for growth become limitless. The investment to prepare and pass the exam pays dividends across your lifetime. So take the first step and commit to becoming certified!

How to Use This Guide

Diving headfirst into exam preparation can be an overwhelming experience, even for the most seasoned professionals. Navigating through the myriad of concepts, theories, and best practices in the field of human resources is far from a walk in the park. However, this guide has been meticulously designed to facilitate a smoother journey toward attaining your SHRM CP or SCP certification. It's a stepping-stone, a beacon, and a strategic partner, all rolled into one.

The primary aim of this guide is to provide a comprehensive and clear pathway for your exam preparation. It's less about cramming last-minute facts and more about understanding the key concepts and real-world applications of human resource management. This guide is your ally, designed to provide you with the tools necessary to not only pass the exam but also enrich your professional expertise.

Each chapter in this guide is dedicated to a different aspect of the SHRM Body of Competency and Knowledge (BoCK). The chapters begin with a theoretical overview of the topic, followed by its practical applications and relevance in today's HR landscape. Theories and concepts are explained in simple, accessible language, making it easier to grasp complex ideas. The chapters also include real-life examples and case studies to illustrate how these theories play out in the real world.

The end of each chapter contains a set of practice questions with detailed answers. These are designed to test your understanding of the chapter and provide a taste of what to expect in the actual exam. Be sure to review these questions and understand why the correct answers are right and why the wrong ones are not. This practice will enhance your reasoning skills, a critical requirement for the situational judgment questions in the SHRM CP and SCP exams.

This guide is not meant to be digested in a single sitting, nor should it be used as a last-minute cramming tool. Instead, think of it as a marathon, not a sprint. Plan your study schedule so that you can go through each chapter in detail, giving yourself enough time to understand and assimilate the information. Regular, consistent study sessions are more effective than long, infrequent ones.

While going through the guide, it's essential to take notes. Jot down key points, make flashcards of critical concepts, or create diagrams to visualize theories. These notes will be your quick-revision tools as the exam date approaches.

Study Tips and Strategies

Preparing for the SHRM-CP or SHRM-SCP exam takes time, dedication, and the right study techniques. With some strategic planning and preparation, you can pass with flying colors. This chapter provides tips and advice for developing an effective study plan based on your learning style and priorities.

Start by realistically assessing how much time you can devote to studying each week, so you can design a schedule accordingly. Most exam prep requires 60-100 hours over at least 3-6 months for success. Give yourself enough lead time before your planned exam date to cover all the material without rushing.

Once you know your timeframe, determine your available hours for studying per week. Calendar out a consistent schedule that creates accountability yet retains flexibility for your lifestyle. Block out study sessions in advance to make them a priority amidst work and life demands. Planning is key.

Next, analyze your strengths and weaknesses to focus your study plan. Closely review the SHRM content outline and Body of Competency & Knowledge (BoCK) to identify your weakest knowledge domains or topic areas. Allocate more time upfront to thoroughly learn these subjects and seek additional resources or training if needed.

As you study, make frequent use of self-assessments to evaluate your progress. SHRM's practice tests available in the prep tool kit provide a good benchmark for what to expect on the real exam. Repeat practice tests on your weak areas until you achieve mastery.

Carefully read rationales for each question, even those you answer correctly. Understanding why choices are right or wrong improves critical thinking. And compile any unclear concepts into a list for further review.

Tailor your study methods to your personal learning style. Auditory learners may prefer podcasts or lectures. Visual learners tend to find charts, diagrams, and images most helpful. Kinesthetic or experiential learners will want to apply concepts in real scenarios. Know your preferences so you can optimize techniques.

Many learners benefit from a blend. Outline critical takeaways, draw process flowcharts, take notes by hand, listen to SHRM's audio study sessions – employ varied approaches for well-rounded comprehension. Teaching concepts to others or creating sample exam questions further cements retention.

The SHRM Learning System provides structured curriculum including textbooks, online modules, and thousands of practice questions to build knowledge foundation. Supplement with other reputable prep programs or textbooks for a change of pace and viewpoint diversity.

Some find creating study groups or finding mentors valuable for collaboration, accountability, and discussing challenges. But beware study fatigue – take breaks to recharge when needed. Adjust your plan over time based on results.

Make the most of small study pockets by keeping flashcards or practice questions handy for quick review during down moments. Test yourself everywhere to maximize repetition of key facts across study mediums.

In final weeks before your exam date, focus intensely on practice exams under timed conditions. The SHRM online simulators mimic real testing environments, mixing in experimental unscored items. Analyze each practice test result to identify lingering gaps for last minute review.

In summary, allow sufficient preparation time for the SHRM certification exams and develop a personalized study plan tailored to your needs and learning preferences. Consistency, self-assessment, and employing varied techniques will help optimize your retention and confidence leading up to test day. With the right preparation, you can pass the SHRM-CP or SHRM-SCP exam and advance your HR career. Best of luck with your studies!

Understanding the Exam Format

Familiarity with the format of an exam is in itself a game-changer. It's like having a map when you're navigating new territory. The SHRM CP and SCP exams have a distinctive structure that reflects their focus on the practical application of HR knowledge and competencies. Understanding this format will give you a substantial advantage as you dive into your exam preparation.

The SHRM CP and SCP exams consist of 160 multiple-choice questions each, divided into two types: Knowledge Items and Situational Judgment Items. Each of these item types contributes equally to your total score, with Knowledge Items forming 60% and Situational Judgment Items comprising the remaining 40%.

Knowledge Items, as the term suggests, are designed to test your understanding of factual information. These cover the technical competency areas in the SHRM Body of Competency and Knowledge (BoCK), namely People, Organization, Workplace, and Strategy. These questions may require you to recall specific facts or understand the application of theories and processes. Some questions might ask you to choose the best definition of a term, while others might require you to select the correct step in a process.

On the other hand, Situational Judgment Items present you with realistic work scenarios and ask you to choose the best course of action from the options provided. These questions assess your understanding of the behavioral competencies in the SHRM BoCK, including Leadership & Navigation, Ethical Practice, Business Acumen, Relationship Management, Consultation, Critical Evaluation, Global & Cultural Effectiveness, and Communication. These scenarios often have more than one correct answer, but your job is to select the most effective response according to SHRM's guidelines and best practices.

Both exams span four hours, providing ample time to answer all questions without rushing. The exams are computer-administered and are conducted in secure testing centers. The question distribution across the various competency areas is based on the guidelines provided by SHRM. It's essential to review these guidelines to understand which areas contribute more to your score.

Once you begin the exam, you can navigate between questions, flag questions for review, and change your answers within the given time. It's advisable to review your flagged questions if time permits, but remember, there's no penalty for guessing, so it's better to answer all questions, even if you're unsure.

Business Acumen and Communication in HR

Understanding Business Functions

For HR to effectively support organizational goals, human resource professionals must have a strong grasp of core business functions and how they interact. This chapter provides an overview of key business operations across departments that HR should comprehend, and how to apply that knowledge strategically.

Finance
The finance or accounting team manages cash flow, budgeting, asset management, investments, payroll, audits, taxes, and financial reporting. As business partners, HR collaborates on workforce budgeting and payroll while ensuring compliance with accounting regulations. Knowledge of financial analysis helps HR provide metrics-driven talent management.

Marketing
The marketing department develops strategies to promote sales and brand awareness through advertising, campaigns, social media, events, pricing models, and market research. HR supports marketing by ensuring optimal staffing, training for campaigns, analyzing customer data, and monitoring brand sentiment related to company culture.

Sales
The sales department converts leads into customers and revenue through pipelines, presentations, relationship building, optimizing conversions, and understanding buyer motivations. HR enables sales by sourcing talent, providing training on consultative skills, and designing compensation incentives around revenue or renewals.

Customer Service
Customer service teams support and retain customers through onboarding, troubleshooting, education, engagement, and measuring satisfaction via surveys or NPS scores. HR policies impact the customer experience through hiring practices, training, and performance management focused on service excellence.

Operations
Operations refers to the core business production processes that deliver the product or service. HR develops standards for production workers, oversees safety procedures, measures process efficiency, and ensures adequate staffing during fluctuations.

Research and Development
Research & development (R&D) involves creating innovative new products/services and enhancing current offerings. HR aids R&D by recruiting scientists, designers, engineers, overseeing intellectual property protections, and facilitating collaboration across creative teams.

Legal/Compliance
Legal and compliance departments minimize risk by ensuring adherence to regulations, protecting IP, overseeing contracts and disputes, and managing corporate governance. HR must partner closely with legal/compliance on policies, employment law, data security, investigations, and training.

Information Technology
IT focuses on building and supporting technology infrastructure and systems that power operations through hardware, software, networking, cybersecurity and helpdesk support. HR relies on IT for applicant tracking, HRIS system management, and effectively using data while assisting IT with talent acquisition and skills training.

Facilities/Real Estate
Facilities, construction, and real estate departments oversee physical offices, warehouses, infrastructure build-outs, equipment, leasing, and property management. HR coordinates with these teams on office layouts, ergonomics, parking, event spaces, and access controls to enable a productive workplace.

Supply Chain/Logistics
Supply chain focuses on end-to-end process of transporting and supplying components or products, managing vendors, forecasting, warehouses, fleets, shipping, and inventory control. HR ensures hiring and compliance within this complex web of global operations and strategic partnerships.

Above are ten business functions HR support through specialized understanding. There are other support departments HR coordinates with such as marketing, PR, business development, procurement/purchasing, and program management offices. The larger the organization, the more business functions involved.

Remember that every department shares a common mission to foster company success. Seeing the interconnectivity between all business units allows HR to align policies and initiatives across the enterprise and act as a strategic enabler. Learning core operations beyond just HR enables true partnership.

HR's Role in Strategy

Strategy and human resources (HR) are two distinct yet interconnected aspects of an organization. When these two forces work hand-in-hand, they can propel an organization towards its goals and ensure sustained growth. Understanding HR's role in strategy is critical not only for HR professionals but also for leaders across the organization.

In the past, HR was often viewed as a largely administrative function, dealing with hiring, payroll, benefits, and compliance. Today, however, the role of HR has significantly evolved. Modern HR professionals are strategic partners who play a crucial role in shaping and executing the organization's strategy.

HR contributes to strategy in several significant ways. First, it aligns the workforce with the organization's strategic goals. This alignment involves ensuring that the right people with the right skills are in the right roles at the right time. It involves talent acquisition, talent management, succession planning, and workforce planning. By managing these aspects effectively, HR ensures that the organization has the human capital needed to achieve its strategic objectives.

Second, HR plays a key role in developing the organization's culture, which is a critical factor in strategy implementation. Culture shapes behavior within the organization and influences how strategies are executed. HR influences culture through various means, including leadership development, performance management, reward systems, and communication.

Third, HR helps build organizational capabilities that are crucial for strategic success. These capabilities include leadership, innovation, agility, and collaboration. Through initiatives such as training and development, performance management, and organizational design, HR helps develop these capabilities and embed them into the organization's DNA.

Additionally, HR acts as a bridge between the organization's strategy and its employees. It communicates the strategy to employees, helps them understand their role in it, and engages them towards its execution. This role is critical because employees are the ones who bring the strategy to life.

However, for HR to effectively contribute to strategy, it needs to understand the business deeply. HR professionals should be familiar with the organization's industry, competitors, market trends, and customer needs. They should understand the organization's strategic goals, the challenges in achieving them, and how their work can contribute to overcoming these challenges.

Moreover, HR needs to speak the language of the business. It should be able to articulate its contributions in terms of business outcomes, such as profitability, customer satisfaction, and market share. This ability helps HR gain credibility and influence in the organization and ensures its contributions to strategy are recognized and valued.

Effective Communication in HR

Communication serves as the lifeblood of organizations. As HR professionals, strong communication skills are essential for educating, informing, influencing, and connecting across all levels and functions. This chapter provides best practices for mastering HR communication strategies and optimizing information flow.

Active Listening
Active listening demonstrates genuine interest and facilitates understanding. When colleagues speak, give them your undivided attention. Maintain eye contact, ask thoughtful follow-up questions, paraphrase key points, and avoid interrupting. These behaviors encourage openness and relationship building.

Succinct Writing
Write emails, reports, and correspondence as succinctly as possible while still including critical details. Get to the point quickly. Favor short sentences and paragraphs focused on one topic. Proofread to eliminate wordiness or redundancies. Leaders appreciate brevity.

Impactful Presentations
When presenting to groups, craft a clear narrative flow using storytelling techniques. Limit text-dense slides and incorporate visuals, examples, and audience interactions. Practice aloud to refine your pacing, tone, and body language. Tailor your content and style to the audience. Send post-presentation follow-up summaries.

Constructive Feedback Delivery
Feedback presented positively promotes growth. Use the Situation-Behavior-Impact model: Describe the situation objectively, be specific about observed behaviors, and explain the business impact both positive and negative. Allow the recipient to share their perspective and co-create solutions. Follow up.

Cross-Department Collaboration

Proactively share HR initiatives with other departments and incorporate their feedback. Develop relationships company-wide through meetings, events, and networking. This facilitates collaboration on policies and programs that support common goals. Stay accessible.

Cultural/Generational Communication

Recognize differing cultural norms and generational values that shape workplace communication styles. Adjust your approach for each audience without making assumptions. Be inclusive by welcoming diverse perspectives. Seek to understand before seeking to be understood.

Change Management Messaging

Major organizational changes require thoughtful communication across all phases of rollout and reinforcement. Share the rationale transparently. Solicit input and address concerns. Convey impacts at the individual level. Celebrate wins and milestones. Communication brings people along.

Crisis Communications

During crises or scandals, HR must partner with leadership and PR to deliver timely, accurate, and reassuring messaging. Express empathy, share known details, outline response plans, and provide resources. Monitor rumor mills and continue transparent communication. This builds resilience.

Executive Presence

Executive presence involves communicating strategically and authoritatively when interfacing with C-suite leaders. Prepare diligently, speak confidently, avoid unnecessary details, summarize takeaways, and follow through reliably. This builds your leadership brand.

Virtual Communication

Remote and hybrid work makes digital communication skills essential. Convey warmth through video conferences by maintaining eye contact and active listening cues. Add some small talk before diving into heavy topics. And stay connected between meetings with brief check-ins.

The best HR professionals have honed both the strategic thinking to shape messaging and the interpersonal skills to connect with audiences authentically. They master both the content and delivery, adjusting their approach based on cultural cues and context. With continuous improvement and intention, you can become an influencer through great communication.

Financial Management in HR

Financial management is a fundamental aspect of any business function, and HR is no exception. HR financial management involves planning, organizing, directing, and controlling the financial activities within the HR department. It ensures that the resources allotted to HR are utilized efficiently and effectively, contributing to the organization's financial health and strategic objectives.

The first element in HR financial management is budgeting. Budgeting is the process of estimating the funds needed for different HR activities such as recruitment, training, benefits, and compensation. A well-crafted budget serves as a roadmap, guiding the department's financial decisions throughout the year. It promotes discipline in spending and helps prevent overruns. HR professionals should be skilled in budgeting and should be able to justify their budget requests based on their contribution to the organization's goals.

Compensation is another major area where HR's financial management plays a crucial role. Designing competitive and equitable compensation packages is a complex task that requires a thorough understanding of labor market trends, organizational strategy, and financial constraints. HR needs to ensure that the compensation structure motivates and retains employees while also aligning with the organization's financial capabilities and strategic objectives.

Benefits management is an area where HR can create significant financial impact. By choosing the right mix of benefits, HR can enhance employee satisfaction and retention while managing costs. HR can leverage various strategies such as benefits pooling, self-insurance, and wellness programs to reduce benefits costs. It can also use benefits analytics to understand the utilization of different benefits and adjust the benefits offering accordingly.

Another aspect of financial management in HR is the measurement and analysis of HR metrics. These metrics, such as cost per hire, turnover cost, training cost per employee, provide insights into the efficiency and effectiveness of HR activities. HR should regularly track and analyze these metrics, use them for decision making, and communicate them to the organization's leadership to demonstrate the value of HR.

Investment in training and development is a significant part of HR's budget. While such investment is essential for enhancing employee skills and performance, it's important to ensure it delivers a reasonable return. HR should evaluate the effectiveness of training programs through methods like reaction surveys, learning assessments, behavior observation, and impact analysis. This evaluation helps HR refine its training initiatives and justify its training investments.

In financial management, HR also needs to ensure compliance with various financial regulations related to HR practices. These regulations may pertain to areas like payroll, tax, benefits, and financial reporting. Non-compliance can result in penalties and can damage the organization's reputation. HR should stay updated on these regulations and incorporate them into its practices.

Managing outsourcing contracts is another area where HR's financial acumen is required. HR often outsources activities like payroll processing, benefits administration, and training. It needs to negotiate and manage these contracts in a way that delivers quality service while controlling costs.

Financial management skills are becoming increasingly important for HR professionals. They enhance HR's credibility, influence, and strategic contribution in the organization. They enable HR to make data-driven decisions, optimize resource utilization, and demonstrate its value. HR professionals should, therefore, strive to develop these skills and apply them in their work.

Practice Questions and Detailed Answers

Understanding business acumen and communication skills are essential for a successful career in HR. To help you assess and improve your knowledge in these areas, here are some practice questions along with detailed answers.

1. **What does business acumen mean in the context of HR, and why is it important?**

Business acumen refers to the ability to understand the organization's business model, industry, and competitive environment, and to use this understanding to make informed decisions. For HR professionals, business acumen means understanding how HR practices contribute to the organization's strategic objectives, profitability, and competitive advantage. It's important because it enhances HR's credibility, influence, and strategic contribution in the organization. It enables HR to align its practices with the organization's goals and to communicate its value in business terms.

2. **How can an HR professional develop business acumen?**

HR professionals can develop business acumen through several ways:

- Learning about the organization's industry, competitors, and customers.

18

- Understanding the organization's business model, strategic goals, and key performance indicators.
- Building relationships with business leaders and understanding their strategic needs.
- Participating in cross-functional projects to gain a broader organizational perspective.
- Regularly reading business news and attending industry events.

3. **What are the key elements of effective communication in HR?**

The key elements of effective communication in HR include clarity, consistency, timeliness, listening, and feedback. Clarity means conveying messages in a way that is easy to understand. Consistency involves ensuring that all communications align with each other and with the organization's goals. Timeliness refers to providing information when it's most needed. Listening involves understanding the needs, concerns, and ideas of employees. Feedback means acknowledging the messages received and responding appropriately.

4. **How can HR use communication to facilitate change?**

HR can use communication to facilitate change in several ways:

- Explaining the need for change and its benefits to employees.
- Communicating the change plan and the employees' role in it.
- Addressing employees' concerns and answering their questions.
- Keeping employees updated on the progress of change.
- Encouraging feedback and using it to refine the change process.

5. **How can HR ensure its communication is effective?**

HR can ensure its communication is effective by:

- Planning its communications carefully, considering the message, audience, medium, and timing.
- Using simple and clear language.
- Checking for understanding and asking for feedback.
- Using multiple communication channels to reach all employees.
- Training its staff in effective communication skills.

6. **How can HR use communication to enhance employee engagement?**

HR can use communication to enhance employee engagement by:

- Regularly communicating organizational goals and progress.

- Recognizing employee achievements and contributions.

- Encouraging two-way communication and listening to employees' ideas and concerns.

- Providing timely and constructive feedback.

- Ensuring transparency in HR policies and decisions.

7. **What communication strategies can HR use during a crisis?**

During a crisis, HR can use the following communication strategies:

- **Transparency**: Share as much information as possible, as early as possible. This can help alleviate fear and uncertainty.

- **Consistency**: Ensure that the same message is relayed across all channels to avoid confusion.

- **Frequent Updates**: Keep employees updated on developments and changes in a timely manner.

- **Empathy**: Show understanding and compassion for the challenges and fears employees might be facing.

- **Action Oriented**: Provide clear instructions on what employees need to do.

8. **What role does business acumen play in strategic HR decision-making?**

Business acumen plays a crucial role in strategic HR decision-making in several ways:

- **Alignment**: It aids in aligning HR strategies with business goals.

- **Justification**: It enables HR to justify its decisions in business terms.

- **Influence**: It enhances HR's influence in strategic discussions.

- **Anticipation**: It enables HR to anticipate business needs and develop proactive HR solutions.

- **Measurement**: It helps HR measure and demonstrate its strategic contribution.

9. **How can HR use communication to manage diversity and inclusion in the workplace?**

HR can use communication to manage diversity and inclusion by:

- **Awareness**: Communicating the importance of diversity and inclusion to the organization's success.

- **Policies**: Clearly communicating the organization's diversity and inclusion policies and expectations.

- **Open Dialogue**: Facilitating open and respectful dialogue on diversity and inclusion issues.

- **Training**: Providing training on diversity and inclusion topics.

- **Feedback**: Encouraging and acting on feedback related to diversity and inclusion.

10. **What are some ways to measure the effectiveness of HR's communication?**

The effectiveness of HR's communication can be measured using several methods:

- **Surveys**: Employee surveys can be used to measure their understanding, satisfaction, and feedback regarding HR's communication.

- **Feedback Sessions**: Regular feedback sessions can provide qualitative insights into the effectiveness of communication.

- **Readership/Viewership Metrics**: For digital communications, readership or viewership metrics can show how many employees are accessing the communication.

- **Action Taken**: The actions taken by employees in response to communication can indicate its effectiveness.

Consultation and Critical Evaluation

The Role of HR Consultants

HR consultants bring specialized expertise to organizations seeking to improve their human resource strategies and capabilities. They provide an outside perspective to identify areas for enhancement and help implement solutions tailored to the company's needs. This chapter explores the multifaceted role of HR consultants as change agents.

Strategic Advisors
HR consultants often serve as strategic advisors, partnering with an organization's leadership team to align talent management with overarching business objectives. They review current HR initiatives against industry best practices to identify gaps and opportunities. Strategic plans are then co-created to foster a high-performing workforce.

Culture Diagnosticians
Assessing and shaping workplace culture is another common role for HR consultants. They conduct organizational analysis to diagnose the existing culture including its values, norms, and unwritten rules. Cultural evolution is plotted to determine needed interventions towards a desired future state reflecting company values and brand identity.

Compliance Experts
HR consultants are well-versed in ever-evolving employment laws and regulations affecting the workplace. They can effectively assess compliance risks in areas like equal employment opportunity, harassment prevention, or wage and hour policies. Consultants recommend updates to ensure legal obligations are met, company liability is limited, and employees are protected.

Talent Evaluators
HR consultants often evaluate workforce talent through skills audits, individual assessments, or analyzing employee performance data. They identify talent gaps, assess capabilities needed to achieve business goals, and provide ideas for upskilling/reskilling. Succession planning is examined and mapped to current and future roles.

Process Mappers
A key aspect of HR consulting involves mapping out and optimizing essential workforce processes in recruitment, onboarding, compensation, performance

management etc. Consultants dissect current workflows and systems to reduce inefficiencies, gaps, or obstacles using Lean and Six Sigma methodologies.

Change Leads

Implementing recommendations requires change adoption across the organization. Consultants serve as change leaders using strategies like stakeholder communication plans, training programs, progress tracking, and coaching to drive and sustain transformation. Their expertise navigates resistant cultures.

Special Project Managers

Organizations often leverage HR consultants for special projects requiring an infusion of skills and bandwidth like large-scale restructures, international expansions, M&A integrations, or technology implementations. Consultants provide seasoned project management through these complex transitions.

Executive Coaches

Some HR consultants take on executive coaching roles to develop leadership capabilities in key individuals. Through personal assessments and regular sessions, coaches unlock leaders' potential by increasing self-awareness, emotional intelligence, strategic thinking, and communication abilities.

Trainers

Many HR consultants have expertise in instructional design and adult learning theories. They work collaboratively to build customized training programs on topics like preventing harassment, leading inclusive teams, optimizing employee engagement, or building presentational skills. Some provide train-the-trainer enablement.

Interim Support

Consultants often serve as interim HR leaders or staff during leadership transitions or temporary talent gaps. They fulfill specialized roles or supplement bandwidth allowing organizations to operate effectively while conducting hiring - a win-win situation.

The breadth of value HR consultants provide stems from their specialized skills, external vantage point, and accumulation of experience across diverse industries and situations. Organizations realize a multiplied return on investment when consultants' guidance is implemented effectively. Partnering with these professionals unlocks transformational growth.

Tools for Critical Evaluation in HR

Making sound decisions in HR relies on critically evaluating information from diverse sources. Various tools and methods exist to facilitate analysis, identify correlations, weigh trade-offs, and select optimal solutions. This chapter will explore useful tools for critical thinking and evidence-based decision making.

Benchmarking
Benchmarking involves comparing your HR metrics and practices against internal goals, past performance, competitors, and industry standards. This reveals performance gaps, future opportunities, and best practices to replicate. Some key benchmarks include turnover, hiring velocity, training hours, compensation, and engagement.

SWOT Analysis
A SWOT analysis allows examining the strengths, weaknesses, opportunities, and threats impacting HR strategies or programs. Strengths and weaknesses represent internal factors within your control. Opportunities and threats are external factors in the environment. SWOT provides a holistic lens.

Cost-Benefit Analysis
Cost-benefit analysis weighs the total expected costs versus total expected benefits of a given HR initiative to determine net value. Both direct and indirect costs like training, technology, administration must be considered against quantified talent, productivity, or revenue gains.

ROI Forecasting
Forecasting the return on investment of programs like learning, diversity efforts, or benefits packages involves estimating the financial payoff from intangible gains like higher engagement scores, reduced turnover, faster promotion rates, or improved productivity. Set measurable outcomes.

Surveys and Assessments
Surveys, assessments, and 360 reviews solicit stakeholder perspectives on HR services, culture, needs, pain points, and ideas. The resulting data informs strategy and tracks progress. Customize questions and analyze trends in responses.

Focus Groups
Facilitated focus groups allow real-time observation of stakeholder attitudes, beliefs, and ideas about a topic. The interaction between participants yields deeper insights. Useful for testing new programs, gaining feedback, or exploring culture.

Statistical Analysis
Applying statistical analysis methods helps make sense of employee datasets, survey results, and metrics. Techniques like correlation, regression, confidence intervals, and hypothesis testing reveal meaningful patterns and support data-driven decisions.

Process Mapping
Detailing end-to-end processes via flowcharts identifies efficiencies, waste, delays, decision points, and dependencies. It illuminates root causes. Later, quantify improvements from process optimization efforts by tracking changes in metrics like time, cost, or quality.

Risk Assessments
Identify potential risks stemming from HR policies and practices such as compliance gaps, litigation exposures, data security vulnerabilities, or brand reputation. Analyze the likelihood and impact of each and define mitigation strategies based on risk appetite.

Pilot Programs
Pilot testing new programs on a small scale provides real-world data on results and risks before full investment. Pilots allow refinements to be made. Gradually expand once the concept proves successful.

No single tool provides a complete picture. Combining benchmarking, cost/benefit analysis, surveying, focus groups, statistical analysis and other techniques creates a comprehensive fact base for critical decision making and continuous improvement. Wield these tools to sharpen your HR strategies.

Data-Driven Decision Making

Data-driven decision making is becoming increasingly important in today's business world. It involves making decisions based on solid data and analytical insights rather than intuition or observation alone. This chapter will equip you with the knowledge and insights to harness the power of data for making informed decisions.

The first step to incorporating data-driven decision making in your operations involves understanding what kind of data is relevant to your goals. Different types of data including qualitative data (e.g., customer reviews, employee feedback) and quantitative data (e.g., sales figures, website traffic metrics) can provide invaluable insights. The key is to identify the data that directly correlates with your business objectives.

Next, it's crucial to develop a system for collecting and storing this data. This could involve anything from sophisticated data management software to simple spreadsheets, depending on the nature and scale of your operations. Regardless of the method, the goal is to ensure that the data is accurately captured and easily accessible for analysis.

Analyzing the collected data is where the magic happens. Data analysis can be as simple as identifying trends over time or as complex as using machine learning algorithms to make predictions about future behavior. The level of analysis will depend on your business needs and the resources you have at your disposal. Remember, the goal is to extract actionable insights from the data that can inform your decision-making process.

After gathering insights from the data, it's time to make decisions. Data-driven decision making isn't just about following what the data says blindly. It's about using the data as one piece of the puzzle. Consider the context, potential implications, and your business instincts along with the data to make balanced decisions.

It's important to note that data-driven decision making is not a one-time process. It's an ongoing cycle of collecting data, analyzing it, making decisions, and then collecting more data to assess the impact of those decisions. This cycle allows you to continuously learn, adapt, and improve.

Problem-Solving Techniques in HR

HR professionals frequently encounter ambiguous problems involving complex human dynamics and multi-faceted organizational challenges. Mastering structured approaches to unravel issues and identify innovative solutions is an invaluable skillset. This chapter outlines techniques to enhance analytical thinking and decision-making.

Defining the Problem
It seems obvious, but taking time to thoroughly define the problem is critical. Consider impacts across the employee lifecycle – hiring, onboarding, development, retention, separation. Clarify objectives, isolate root causes, and set a clear problem statement.

Gathering Data

Problems are best solved with evidence, not assumptions. Take an investigative approach to gather relevant qualitative and quantitative data through surveys, focus groups, benchmarking, process mapping, and data analysis. Supplement with research on best practices.

Analyzing Alternatives

With foundational understanding established, brainstorm a range of potential solutions both conventional and unconventional. List pros and cons for each alternative and compare against objectives. Seek input from stakeholders. Evaluating different lenses prevents narrow solutions.

Evaluating Trade-Offs

HR issues often present trade-offs between competing interests like cost versus impact or speed versus quality. Aim for the optimal balance - maximize key gains without unacceptable sacrifices. Quantify trade-offs where possible.

PILOT Testing

Before full-scale implementation, pilot test shortlisted solutions on a small sample group to gather empirical insights. PILOTs enable refinement of the concept, highlight potential pitfalls, and provide proof points to build stakeholder buy-in.

Managing Resistance

Inevitably, substantive changes face some resistance from those adverse to adjustment or with misconceptions. Anticipate and understand objections. Craft targeted communication and allow input to increase adoption. Work through resistance gently but firmly.

Implementation Planning

Meticulously plan the rollout details including timing, required resources, communications, training, process changes, measurement systems and contingencies. Collaborate cross-functionally. Plan the work, work the plan.

Progress Tracking

Once implemented, systematically track solution effectiveness using established metrics and benchmarks. Monitor leading and lagging indicators, adjust course as needed, recognize achievements, and identify ongoing opportunities for improvement.

Root Cause Corrective Action

If major problems persist, "peel the onion" by repeatedly asking why until the root cause is uncovered. This prevents superficial solutions that mask deeper issues. Address the true root cause for sustained impact.

In summary, integrating analytics, creativity and project management in a structured framework leads to optimal problem-solving. Rushing to solutions without careful analysis of root causes and potential impacts often backfires. Take time to strategically define, assess, pilot, implement, monitor and refine. The reward is sustainable solutions for engaging talent.

Practice Questions and Detailed Answers

Consultation and critical evaluation are key competencies for HR professionals. They enable HR professionals to guide organizational decisions and to assess the effectiveness of HR initiatives. To help you improve these competencies, let's explore some practice questions and their detailed answers.

1. **What does consultation mean in an HR context?**

In the HR context, consultation means partnering with business leaders to align HR practices with business objectives, solve people-related business problems, and enhance organizational performance. It involves understanding business needs, offering expert advice, facilitating decision-making, and leading or supporting the implementation of solutions.

2. **What skills are necessary for effective consultation in HR?**

Effective consultation in HR requires several skills:

- **Business Acumen**: Understanding the organization's business model, industry, and strategic objectives.
- **HR Expertise**: Strong knowledge of HR practices and principles.
- **Problem-Solving**: The ability to analyze problems, generate solutions, and make decisions.
- **Influence**: The ability to gain support and commitment from stakeholders.
- **Communication**: The ability to convey information and ideas effectively.

3. **What does critical evaluation mean in an HR context?**

In the HR context, critical evaluation means assessing the effectiveness and efficiency of HR practices based on data and evidence. It involves defining success measures, collecting and analyzing data, drawing conclusions, and making recommendations for improvement.

4. **What skills are necessary for effective critical evaluation in HR?**

29

Effective critical evaluation in HR requires several skills:

- **Analytical Skills**: The ability to collect, analyze, and interpret data.

- **Critical Thinking**: The ability to question assumptions, identify biases, and make logical and sound judgments.

- **Business Acumen**: Understanding the business impact of HR practices.

- **Communication**: The ability to present findings and recommendations in a clear and compelling manner.

5. **How can an HR professional develop consultation skills?**

HR professionals can develop consultation skills through several ways:

- **Learning**: Enhancing their knowledge of business and HR practices.

- **Practice**: Applying consultation skills in their work, and learning from their experiences.

- **Feedback**: Seeking feedback on their consultation skills from colleagues and clients.

- **Mentorship or Coaching**: Learning from experienced consultants.

- **Training or Education**: Participating in consultation skills training or education.

6. **How can an HR professional develop critical evaluation skills?**

HR professionals can develop critical evaluation skills through several ways:

- **Learning**: Enhancing their knowledge of analytics, research methods, and critical thinking.

- **Practice**: Applying critical evaluation skills in their work, and learning from their experiences.

- **Feedback**: Seeking feedback on their critical evaluation skills from colleagues and clients.

- **Mentorship or Coaching**: Learning from experienced evaluators.

- **Training or Education**: Participating in critical evaluation skills training or education.

7. **How can consultation support organizational change?**

Consultation can support organizational change by:

- **Needs Assessment**: Identifying the need for change and defining the desired outcomes.

- **Solution Design**: Designing change initiatives that align with the organization's strategy and culture.

- **Stakeholder Engagement**: Gaining support and commitment from stakeholders.

- **Implementation Support**: Guiding and supporting the implementation of change.

- **Evaluation**: Assessing the impact of change and making necessary adjustments.

8. **How can critical evaluation contribute to continuous improvement in HR?**

Critical evaluation can contribute to continuous improvement in HR by:

- **Effectiveness Assessment**: Assessing the impact of HR practices on organizational performance.

- **Efficiency Analysis**: Analyzing the cost-effectiveness of HR practices.

- **Best Practice Benchmarking**: Comparing HR practices with those of leading organizations.

- **Gap Identification**: Identifying areas of improvement in HR practices.

- **Recommendation**: Making evidence-based recommendations for improvement.

9. **What are some common challenges in HR consultation and how can they be addressed?**

Some common challenges in HR consultation include resistance to change, lack of business knowledge, and limited influence. These can be addressed by:

- **Resistance to Change**: Encouraging open communication, involving employees in decision-making, and providing support during the change process.

- **Lack of Business Knowledge**: Enhancing business acumen through learning, networking, and participation in business projects.

- **Limited Influence**: Building credibility through expertise, results, and relationship-building.

10.   **What are some common challenges in HR critical evaluation and how can they be addressed?**

Some common challenges in HR critical evaluation include lack of data, limited analytical skills, and resistance to findings. These can be addressed by:

- **Lack of Data**: Implementing HR information systems, promoting a data culture, and collaborating with other departments to access necessary data.

- **Limited Analytical Skills**: Enhancing analytical skills through training, practice, and learning from experienced evaluators.

- **Resistance to Findings**: Presenting findings in a clear and compelling manner, involving stakeholders in the evaluation process, and focusing on solutions rather than problems.

Ethical Practice and Cultural Effectiveness

Ethics in HR Management

HR professionals serve as the moral compass for organizations when it comes to people practices. Upholding ethical principles earns trust in the workplace and beyond. This chapter provides guidance on ethical decision-making, policies, culture, and common ethical dilemmas faced in HR roles.

Establishing Values

Codify the values and behaviors reflective of the organization's ethical aspirations. These become guideposts for everyday choices. Values might encompass integrity, accountability, compassion, diversity, sustainability, etc. Make sure leadership models expected behaviors.

Written Policies

Develop clear written policies that align to the organization's values on topics like anti-discrimination, anti-harassment, data privacy, absence reporting, internet usage, expenses, and more. Ensure accessibility and enforce consistently at all levels. Update as needed.

Training Content

Incorporate case studies, scenarios and discussions of ethics into employee training programs. Challenge people to explore gray areas and complex situations. Provide resources for speaking up about concerns. Training establishes shared language and expectations.

Modeling From the Top

Leaders, founders, and executives must exemplify ethical conduct since their actions powerfully shape norms. Behaviors like honesty, accountability, empathy and respect for others' perspectives must start at the top to permeate downward.

Anonymous Reporting

Provide anonymous channels for employees to seek advice on or report ethical issues without fear of retaliation. Publish the steps for investigation. Leaders must handle reports with gravity, care and communication.

Addressing Misconduct

Act swiftly when ethical breaches occur. The response should fit the severity of the violation. Involve HR immediately. For severe cases, conduct fair investigations and consider termination. Apply progressive discipline for minor issues.

Rewarding Integrity

Celebrate cases where people demonstrate ethical behavior under pressure, especially when it conflicts with self-interest. Storytelling of "ethics heroes" reinforces priorities. Ethics can factor into performance management.

Asking Guiding Questions

When facing ambiguous situations, ask questions like: Is it legal? Is it consistent with our values? Does it feel right? How would it look publicly? Does it protect our people? Get perspectives beyond your own.

Considering Conflicts

Identify potential conflicts of interest in relationships or business dealings and how to navigate. Disclose relationships to avoid perceptions of bias. Avoid abusing authority in ways that benefit yourself or associates.

Balancing Stakeholders

Ethical pressures often arise when stakeholder interests conflict. Transparency, communication and fairness govern balancing employee welfare with business necessities, legal obligations and customer expectations.

Avoiding Unconscious Bias

Examine decisions for subtle biases related to gender, race, age, ethnicity, disability etc. that can manifest unconsciously. Seek perspectives of underrepresented groups. Data helps overcome blindspots.

Maintaining Confidentiality

Safeguard sensitive employee information around health, performance, compensation, legal status etc. Follow data privacy protocols. Only access privileged data when expressly needed for the role.

Beyond policies, cultivating an ethical culture requires empowering employees at all levels to take personal responsibility for doing the right thing. With dedication, the HR function can elevate integrity organization-wide.

Promoting a Culture of Integrity

An ethical culture is rooted in a shared commitment to doing the right thing. HR plays a pivotal role in cultivating integrity as an organizational value that guides behaviors and decision-making at all levels. This chapter explores strategies for instilling a culture where integrity is expected, modeled, rewarded, and defended.

Lead by Example

Culture starts at the top. Leaders must consistently model integrity through their words and actions. When the C-suite and managers make decisions based on ethics rather than expediency, it signals priorities down the chain. Hold everyone accountable to shared standards, regardless of rank.

Communicate Expectations

Clearly and frequently communicate behavioral expectations around integrity. For example, "We value honesty and transparency with all stakeholders, even when it is uncomfortable." Simple, repeated messaging from leadership keeps values top of mind. Discuss in onboarding.

Shape Recruiting Messaging

Promote the company's commitment to ethics in employer branding content and during recruiting. This attracts talent that shares these values. Probe candidates' views on real ethical scenarios. Make values alignment central to selection.

Train for Ethical Competence

Train employees in ethical frameworks, case studies, and applying company values to decisions. Focus on moral courage and overcoming rationalizations. Equip people to handle grey areas. Refresh periodically to reinforce an ethical mindset.

Empower Principled Employees

Encourage employees at all levels to constructively challenge concerning behaviors without fear of retaliation. Provide safe channels for voicing issues and asking for guidance. Empower people to act based on their principles.

Reward Ethical Choices

Recognize those who uphold ethical standards at personal cost with rewards, promotions, or public praise. The message must be that doing right leads to concrete benefits while unethical behavior has consequences. Explain disciplinary actions internally.

Audit and Assess Risks

Regularly audit policies, processes, controls and culture for ethical risks. Survey employee sentiment and audit complaint hotlines for issues. Proactively address problem areas through updated training, controls, or policies. Stay vigilant.

Keep Perspective

Remember most ethical missteps arise from human frailties like self-interest, fatigue, or environments of high pressure. While unacceptable, treat integrity lapses as opportunities for remediation and courageous culture shaping.

Protect Whistleblowers

Ensure safe, confidential options for reporting suspected misconduct without fear of retaliation. Promptly and fairly investigate all claims and address root causes. Support whistleblowers even when claims are unfounded to encourage speaking up.

Integrity enables sustainable success and positive impact. An ethical culture is not established overnight but through persistent modeling, communication, and courageous action. With constant nurturing by HR, organizations can unlock higher potential.

Understanding Cultural Differences

Today's globalized business environment brings together employees from diverse cultural and geographic backgrounds. Navigating cross-cultural collaboration requires empathy, adaptability, and nuanced communication skills. This chapter provides guidance on understanding key cultural dimensions and delivering culturally competent HR.

Defining Culture

Culture encompasses the shared values, norms, mindsets, practices, and sense of identity within societies and organizations. It shapes how people communicate, make decisions, manage change, handle conflict, and define success. Culture runs deep.

Mapping Cultural Dimensions

Frameworks like Hofstede's 6-D model categorize national/regional cultures along key dimensions: individualism/collectivism, hierarchy/egalitarian, risk avoidance, masculinity/femininity, long/short-term orientation, and indulgence/restraint.

Other models include Hall and Trompenaars. Mapping cultural dimensions provides perspective.

Understanding Individual Variations

While models are useful lenses, remember that individuals express cultural influences uniquely based on personality, family, experiences and personal values. Make no assumptions. Get to know people as holistic individuals. Ask respectful questions.

Slowing Down Perceptions s instinctively notice differences and categorize. But snap perceptions based on appearance often miss nuances. Train yourself to slow down observations and consciously override stereotyping. Appreciate complexity.

Practicing Cultural Empathy

Perspective-taking expands understanding of culturally-linked behaviors. How would this situation look from their vantage point based on respective norms? Imagining differently fosters non-judgmental empathy amidst disagreement.

Finding Common Ground

Despite differences, certain values and aspirations unite humanity in our shared human experiences – care for family, desire for purpose and respect, achievement, love, humor. Discover these connections.

Adapting Communication Styles

Adapt how you communicate across authority conventions, relationship building, nonverbal cues, expressing dissent, conflict styles, feedback delivery, and meeting protocols. Differences are not deficiencies. Modify gracefully.

Contextualizing Feedback

Criticism and direct negative feedback can hold different meanings across cultures. Frame sensitively, add reassurance, discuss indirect modes preferred in local culture, and focus on behaviors not character.

Addressing Culture Clash

When cross-cultural conflicts or misunderstandings arise, facilitate open dialogue from multiple lenses. Aim for understanding, self-reflection about bias, defining shared goals, and reconciling needs.

Learning Foreign Languages

Make an effort to use and learn basic words and phrases in languages spoken by colleagues. This gesture of inclusion helps break down walls and humanize interactions. Ask for help and be patient with yourself.

Navigating Visas/Legalities

Advocate for employee legal accommodations around visas, benefits eligibility, and employment conditions affected by nationality or residency status restrictions. Ensure cultural practices are respected.

HR plays a vital role in cultivating mutual understanding amidst diversity. Approach differences with humility, patience and compassion. Deep listening enables people across cultures to learn from one another and forge an inclusive environment.

Building a Diverse and Inclusive Workplace

Organizations thrive when employees feel welcomed, valued, and able to contribute their full diversity of talents and perspectives. As diversity, equity and inclusion (DEI) partners, HR professionals play a vital role in cultivating a workplace where all can excel. This chapter explores strategies for building diverse, equitable and inclusive cultures.

Lead at the Top

Culture shaping starts with engaged leadership. Leaders must communicate DEI as a business imperative, model inclusive behaviors, hold themselves and others accountable, analyze progress, sponsor employee resource groups (ERGs), and visibly support underrepresented communities.

Write a Vision Statement

Develop a specific vision statement for the organization's diversity and inclusion aspirations endorsed by leadership. This declaration ofintent guides strategic planning. Track progress toward goals over multi-year roadmaps.

Assess the Current Culture

Get baseline data on the existing culture using surveys, focus groups, ERG insights and exit interviews. Look at diversity stats, retention variations, promotion rates, compensation equity, trust in leadership, and belonging. Pinpoint strengths, gaps and pain points.

Update Talent Processes

Examine where bias can influence talent systems like job descriptions, recruiting, interviews, performance reviews, succession planning and selections. Implement anonymized resume screening, diverse slates, structured interviews, job competencies, and balanced panels.

Offer Bias Training

Require everyone to complete unconscious bias training. Have leaders participate in more intensive anti-racism and allyship workshops. Training builds self-awareness and skills for constructive conversations. Include in onboarding.

Support ERGs

Resource and empower employees to launch ERGs focused on identities like race, ethnicity, gender, sexual orientation, disability, veterans and cultural backgrounds. ERGs foster community, professional growth, advocacy and perspectives for the business.

Sponsor Mentorship

Develop formal mentorship and sponsorship initiatives that thoughtfully match mentees/protégés with mentors/sponsors based on needs, backgrounds and experiences. This provides growth opportunities and support.

Highlight Role Models

Amplify stories of diversity role models from underrepresented groups who have risen into leadership, overcome challenges, or exemplify inclusion. Celebrate their journeys to inspire others. Sponsor rising talent.

Encourage Allyship

Train all employees to become allies who will intervene against bias, advocate for equity, educate themselves, and leverage their privilege and voice to defend underrepresented groups. Allies are force multipliers.

Promote Flexibility

Offer flexible work arrangements to support employees with varying abilities, family structures, cultural practices, and needs. Evaluate requests individually. Monitor utilization to ensure equal access.

Foster an inclusive, diverse culture where employees feel safe to bring their authentic selves. This unlocks innovation and resilience. DEI is a continuous journey of growth, not a destination. With persistence and courage, HR can build workplaces where every employee is valued.

Practice Questions and Detailed Answers

In the realm of business, ethical practice and cultural effectiveness are two intertwined concepts that are crucial for sustainable success. They encompass the behaviors, attitudes, and strategies that foster respect, fairness, diversity, and inclusivity within an organization. Let's explore these concepts further through a series of practice questions and detailed answers.

1. **What does ethical practice mean in a business context?**

Ethical practice in a business context refers to conducting business in a manner that is consistent with societal norms and values. This includes, but is not limited to, honesty, fairness, respect, accountability, and transparency. Ethical practice ensures that an organization's actions are not only legal but also morally acceptable.

2. **Why is ethical practice important in business?**

Ethical practice is important in business for several reasons:

- **Trust**: Ethical practice builds trust among stakeholders, including employees, customers, suppliers, and investors.

- **Reputation**: Ethical practice enhances an organization's reputation, which can lead to competitive advantage.

- **Compliance**: Ethical practice helps to prevent legal issues and penalties related to unethical behavior.

- **Sustainability**: Ethical practice contributes to the social and environmental sustainability of the organization.

3. **What are some strategies for promoting ethical practice in an organization?**

Promoting ethical practice in an organization can involve several strategies:

- **Code of Ethics**: Developing a code of ethics that outlines the organization's values and expectations.

- **Training**: Providing ethics training to employees.

- **Leadership**: Setting a good example of ethical behavior at the leadership level.

- **Reporting Mechanism**: Implementing a mechanism for reporting unethical behavior without fear of retaliation.

- **Rewards and Penalties**: Recognizing ethical behavior and penalizing unethical behavior.

4. **What does cultural effectiveness mean in a business context?**

Cultural effectiveness in a business context refers to the ability of an organization to respect, adapt to, and leverage cultural diversity. This includes understanding and valuing cultural differences, fostering an inclusive environment, and utilizing cultural diversity to enhance organizational performance.

5. **Why is cultural effectiveness important in business?**

Cultural effectiveness is important in business for several reasons:

- **Talent**: Cultural effectiveness attracts and retains diverse talent.

- **Innovation**: Cultural effectiveness stimulates different perspectives and ideas, leading to innovation.

- **Market**: Cultural effectiveness enables the organization to understand and serve diverse markets.

- **Collaboration**: Cultural effectiveness promotes collaboration among diverse teams.

6. **What are some strategies for enhancing cultural effectiveness in an organization?**

Enhancing cultural effectiveness in an organization can involve several strategies:

- **Diversity and Inclusion Policy**: Developing a diversity and inclusion policy that outlines the organization's commitments and actions.

- **Training**: Providing cultural competence training to employees.

- **Leadership**: Demonstrating commitment to cultural effectiveness at the leadership level.

- **Representation**: Ensuring representation of diverse groups at all levels of the organization.

- **Inclusion Practices**: Creating an inclusive environment through fair practices and inclusive communication.

Cultural effectiveness and ethical practice are not standalone concepts but are interconnected. Ethical practice provides a moral foundation for cultural effectiveness, while cultural effectiveness enriches the ethical practice by bringing diverse values and perspectives. Together, they create a powerful synergy that can propel an organization towards sustainable success.

7. How can organizations ensure they are operating ethically on a global scale?

Operating ethically on a global scale can be challenging due to the diverse cultural, legal, and ethical norms across countries. However, organizations can ensure ethical operation by:

- **Global Code of Ethics**: Establishing a global code of ethics that respects universal human rights and ethical standards.

- **Local Adaptation**: Adapting the code of ethics to local norms, as long as it does not contradict universal standards.

- **Training**: Training employees on the global and local ethical standards.

- **Monitoring**: Monitoring ethical compliance across different locations and taking corrective actions as needed.

- **Stakeholder Engagement**: Engaging with local stakeholders to understand their expectations and concerns.

8. What are some challenges in implementing cultural effectiveness and how can they be addressed?

Some challenges in implementing cultural effectiveness include resistance to diversity, stereotyping, and lack of cultural competence. These can be addressed by:

- **Resistance to Diversity**: Promoting the benefits of diversity, involving employees in diversity initiatives, and addressing their concerns.

- **Stereotyping**: Educating employees about the harm of stereotypes and encouraging them to see beyond stereotypes.

- **Lack of Cultural Competence**: Providing cultural competence training and creating opportunities for intercultural interaction.

9. How can ethical practice and cultural effectiveness contribute to corporate social responsibility (CSR)?

Ethical practice and cultural effectiveness are integral to CSR. Ethical practice contributes to CSR by ensuring fair treatment of stakeholders, responsible use of resources, and contribution to societal well-being. Cultural effectiveness contributes to CSR by promoting diversity and inclusion, understanding and serving diverse markets, and respecting local cultures in global operations. Together, they help an organization to fulfill its social responsibilities and create positive social impact.

10. **How can organizations measure their ethical practice and cultural effectiveness?**

Measuring ethical practice and cultural effectiveness can involve both quantitative and qualitative methods:

- **Ethical Practice**: Organizations can measure ethical practice by tracking ethical incidents, conducting ethical climate surveys, and obtaining stakeholder feedback.

- **Cultural Effectiveness**: Organizations can measure cultural effectiveness by tracking diversity metrics, conducting inclusion surveys, and obtaining feedback from diverse groups.

Remember, both ethical practice and cultural effectiveness are journeys, not destinations. They require continuous effort, learning, and improvement. Treat challenges as opportunities for growth, success as encouragement for further effort, and every step as a contribution to a better business and a better world.

Leadership and Navigation

Leadership Styles and Their Impact

Leadership style profoundly influences organizational culture, employee engagement, and performance. HR professionals must comprehend leadership models and characteristics that foster positive environments and drive results. This chapter examines common styles, contexts for effectiveness, and developing a personal leadership approach.

Authoritative
Authoritative leaders drive results through high-performance expectations, accountability, and well-defined rewards and consequences. This style promotes compliance yet risks stifling innovation without proper balance. Best applied to turnarounds or highly urgent contexts.

Participative
Participative leaders involve team members in collaborative decision making, transparency, and consensus building. This unlocks commitment yet can dampen speedy execution. Thrives when employee engagement in change is vital or situations are ambiguous.

Coaching
Coaching-focused leaders develop people through individualized support, delegating stretch assignments, and frequent specific feedback. This builds capabilities over time yet requires significant upfront investment. Ideal for talent development or skill building.

Affiliative
Affiliative leaders cultivate people connection, empathy, and emotional positivity. This nurtures engagement amidst adversity yet risks softening necessary critique. Shines during cultural transitions, burnout, or crises requiring resilience.

Democratic
Democratic leaders decide through majority input and consensus building across the team. This leverages collective wisdom yet allows vocal minorities to dominate or stall action. Excels when buy-in is critical or situations lack precedents.

Pace-Setting
Pace-setting leaders hold themselves and teams to extremely high performance

standards and urgency. This drives immediate outcomes yet risks burnout without reprieve. Thrives in unambiguous turnaround or high-velocity contexts.

Servant

Servant leaders prioritize employee development, wellbeing, and empowerment over organizational goals. This earns tremendous loyalty yet dilutes results-focus. Most impactful for non-profits or community-driven organizations.

Situational

Situational leaders adapt their approach strategically based on each circumstance, issue, and team. This versatility enables optimized responses yet risks perceptions of inconsistent or politically expedient leadership.

Authentic

Authentic leaders ground their style in genuine values, purpose, self-discipline, and care for others. They build trust and model integrity. This inspires commitment and superior long-term performance.

The most effective leaders practice awareness of their innate tendencies and adapt approaches situationally based on the context while retaining core authenticity. There is no singular "best" style. HR helps optimize leadership impact through assessment, coaching, and talent development. With intention, each leader can find their unique influential voice.

Developing Leadership Skills in HR

For HR professionals seeking to advance, cultivating one's leadership capabilities is essential. Beyond domain expertise, growth-oriented HR leaders possess strategic mindsets plus skills to inspire teams, influence stakeholders, and drive change. This chapter outlines development pathways to activate HR's leadership potential.

Understanding Leadership Context

Explore organizational context to discern where leadership opportunities exist and what approaches fit the culture. Does the situation call for a bold vision or incremental influence? Technical mastery or inspirational presence? Tactical delivery or big picture orientation? Adopt methods suitable for the environment.

Expanding Strategic Perspective

Strengthen business acumen across functions to contribute insights that support overall organizational performance. Take lateral development roles. Absorb mentorship from non-HR executives to broaden perspective. Think enterprise-wide, not just about HR priorities.

Leading with Purpose and Values

Anchor leadership presence in a clear purpose and set of values that others can connect with. Authentic leaders guided by ethics and meaning lead through stormy environments with poise. Define your cultural contribution.

Enhancing Communication Skills

Exceptional communication abilities including public speaking, storytelling, active listening, and impactful writing distinguish influential leaders. Seek opportunities to inspire through messaging and simplify complexity for clarity.

Driving Change and Innovation

Lead change skillfully through the inspiration-planning-execution continuum. Pitch compelling visions, strategically plan adoption, empower teams to innovate, and tenaciously steer implementation. Change leadership opens growth opportunities.

Coaching and Developing Others

The best leaders are talent cultivators. Energize people through encouragement, development, and unlocking potential. Delegate challenges. Give timely, constructive feedback. Mentor emerging leaders. Succession planning feeds the pipeline.

Making Courageous Decisions

Leadership frequently requires difficult decisions amidst ambiguity involving trade-offs. Build courage and principles to make the right call with conviction even when unpopular. Communicate decisions transparently.

Collaborating Across Groups

Bring together diverse stakeholders to accomplish shared goals through matrix management, collaborative structures, and consultative processes. Bridge differences and build trust in teams to generate collective power.

Driving Results

At the end of the day, leaders must deliver tangible results. Set clear metrics and accountability. Course correct consistently. Celebrate wins. Strive for operational excellence in execution paired with bold vision. Outcomes build credibility.

Leadership capabilities strengthen over time through continually seeking challenges, learning from experience, and developing self-awareness. HR professionals committed to growth can build fulfilling leadership careers guided by purpose.

Navigating Organizational Change

Change is constant in today's organizations. As strategic partners, HR professionals play critical roles in navigating workforce transitions, driving adoption, and sustaining momentum. This chapter explores change management frameworks, strategies, and competencies for leading successful transformations.

Clarifying the Change Vision
Leaders must paint a vivid picture of the future state and reasons for change. What problems will this solve? How will work improve? Appealing to hearts and minds inspires engagement in the vision. Share consistently across channels.

Assessing Impacts
Analyze who will be impacted, how their roles will change, what skills may become obsolete, and what resistance factors exist. Different groups have varying needs for communication and support. Address their perspectives in plans.

Building a Diverse Coalition
A cross-functional coalition representing diverse groups provides broader input, lends credibility, and enables two-way information flow. This core team helps guide strategies tailored to each area while sharing progress.

Executing Pilots
Pilot changes on a small scale to test effectiveness and refine ahead of companywide rollout. Use iterative PDSA (plan-do-study-act) cycles to evaluate outcomes. Gather lessons learned and success stories.

Developing Competencies
Training, coaching, job rotations, and mentorship help build skills required for the change like using new systems, processes, or leadership capabilities. Assess gaps proactively and provide resources.

Communicating Strategically
Transparent communication addressing "how" and "why" enables understanding.

Share timelines, milestone markers, anticipated impacts, and resources. Use multiple channels and encourage two-way discussion.

Securing Early Wins
Early successes build confidence and adoption momentum for larger initiatives. Pursue some quick but meaningful wins to achieve while executing longer term solutions. Celebrate and publicize results.

Monitoring Progress
Establish metrics and milestones to track progress. Watch for lagging indicators like morale or productivity declines and get ahead of issues. Adapt and reinforce expectations to drive sustainability.

Recognizing Contributions
Acknowledge teams and individuals making the change successful through awards, events, town halls, and internal promotion. This reinforces continuance of desired attitudes and efforts.

Managing Resistance
Address resistance head on through listening to concerns, providing forums for input, emphasizing benefits, and coaching those struggling. Maintain composure, patience and understanding.

Change activates HR's strengths in culture shaping, communications, training, and relationship building across the organization. While unsettling, workforce transitions focused on people ultimately fuel success. HR leaders able to navigate these rapids skillfully make an enduring impact.

HR's Role in Vision and Strategy

Organizations rely on HR to attract, develop, and inspire the talent that brings business strategies to life. Beyond efficient operations, forward-thinking HR leaders play a pivotal role in shaping the vision and participating in strategic planning. This chapter explores how HR contributes unique human capital perspectives while executing on strategy.

Understanding the Business

HR cannot strategize in a vacuum. Take the time to learn the broader business model, industry landscape, competitors, challenges, and external trends. Understand key strategic priorities and how the workforce enables them. Identify gaps.

50

Providing Market Insights

Leverage HR's data and touchpoints with employees and candidates to uncover talent-related risks, opportunities, and innovations. Provide insights on workforce demographics, availability, costs, engagement levels, and capability development needed to realize strategic vision.

Collaborating on Vision

When organizational purpose and future vision are articulated, ensure people priorities are reflected. Ask - does our vision allow us to attract and engage the talent we need? Contribute thoughtful perspectives on crafting a compelling vision.

Planning for Disruption

Help assess threats of disruption from technology, competitors, pandemics, and other forces. Identify people risks and opportunities these represent. Offer ideas for proactive workforce planning, upskilling, and adaptation.

Prioritizing HR Investments

Consider all talent programs through a strategic lens by evaluating how strongly each builds competitive advantage versus simply keeping pace. Advocate for human capital investments that accelerate strategy even during tough budgets.

Developing Leaders

Coach and develop leaders on embracing their role communicating strategy and vision to teams. Help equip them with storytelling and culture-shaping skills. Leadership alignment enables consistent contextualization of day-to-day work.

Realigning HR Priorities

Critically evaluate existing HR priorities and projects against strategic goals. Be willing to stop less crucial work streams to focus on the people capabilities most vital to strategic success. Say no where needed.

Raising Risk Flags

If people risks around engagement, culture, or capabilities threaten strategy delivery, boldly voice concerns. Escalate factual data and options for mitigating risks. Take a stand for talent outcomes critical to performance.

Tracking Metrics

Design HR metrics and analytics that provide insights into progress on strategic talent goals such as sourcing specialized skills, improving quality of hire, reducing turnover in key roles, and building bench strength. Report regularly.

Celebrating Milestones

Find creative ways for employees to share in strategy implementation milestones when talent efforts deliver on key business goals. These small celebrations maintain momentum.

With a strategic seat at the table, HR leaders play an invaluable role in developing visionary yet realistic strategies enabled by empowered people. Turn strategy into actionable reality through your team's passion and capabilities.

Practice Questions and Detailed Answers

Leadership and navigation are two foundational pillars of successful management. Leadership is about guiding, inspiring, and influencing people, while navigation is about charting the course and making strategic decisions. Let's delve deeper into these concepts with a set of practice questions and detailed answers.

1. **What are the key qualities of effective leadership?**

Effective leadership transcends beyond managing tasks. It involves:

- **Vision**: Leaders have a clear vision and they can articulate this vision to their team.

- **Empathy**: Leaders understand and resonate with the feelings of their team members.

- **Resilience**: Leaders remain steady and focused, especially in times of crisis.

- **Integrity**: Leaders uphold ethical standards and act with honesty.

- **Influential**: Leaders can motivate and inspire their team towards achieving common goals.

2. **How can one develop leadership skills?**

Developing leadership skills is a continuous process that involves:

- **Self-awareness**: Understanding your strengths and weaknesses.

- **Learning**: Reading leadership books, attending workshops, and learning from mentors.

- **Practice**: Applying learned skills in real-life scenarios.

- **Feedback**: Seeking feedback and making necessary improvements.

- **Reflection**: Regularly reflecting on your actions and their outcomes.

3. **What does navigation mean in a business context?**

In a business context, navigation refers to the ability to set strategic direction, make informed decisions, and steer the organization towards its goals. It involves understanding the business environment, identifying opportunities and threats, and aligning resources and efforts towards the strategic objectives.

4. **Why is navigation important in leadership?**

Navigation is important in leadership because:

- **Direction**: It provides a clear direction for the organization.

- **Decision-making**: It informs decision-making at all levels.

- **Alignment**: It helps align the organization's resources and efforts.

- **Performance**: It enhances the organization's performance and competitiveness.

5. **How can one develop navigation skills?**

Developing navigation skills can involve:

- **Business Acumen**: Understanding the business environment and mastering business tools and techniques.

- **Strategic Thinking**: Cultivating the ability to think strategically and foresee long-term implications.

- **Decision-making**: Improving decision-making skills through practice and learning.

- **Learning from Experience**: Learning from past successes and failures.

6. **How can leadership and navigation work together?**

Leadership and navigation work together in several ways:

- **Vision and Direction**: Leadership provides the vision, and navigation provides the direction to realize that vision.

- **Motivation and Strategy**: Leadership motivates the team, and navigation develops the strategy to channel that motivation.

- **Culture and Alignment**: Leadership shapes the culture, and navigation ensures alignment of the culture with the strategic objectives.

7. **What are some challenges in leadership and navigation and how can they be addressed?**

Challenges in leadership and navigation can include resistance to change, lack of clarity, and misalignment. These can be addressed by:

- **Resistance to Change**: Communicating the need for change, involving stakeholders in the change process, and managing the transition effectively.

- **Lack of Clarity**: Articulating the vision and direction clearly and regularly.

- **Misalignment**: Ensuring alignment of the team, resources, and efforts with the strategic objectives.

8. **How can leadership and navigation contribute to organizational success?**

Leadership and navigation contribute to organizational success by:

- **Culture**: Building a positive and effective culture.

- **Performance**: Enhancing organizational performance and competitiveness.

- **Change Management**: Leading and managing change effectively.

- **Sustainability**: Ensuring the sustainability of the organization.

9. **How can organizations support the development of leadership and navigation skills?**

Organizations can support the development of leadership and navigation skills by:

- **Training and Development**: Providing training and development opportunities.

- **Mentorship**: Establishing mentorship programs.

- **Opportunities**: Creating opportunities for employees to practice these skills.

- **Support**: Providing necessary resources and support.

10.   **What role does continuous learning play in leadership and navigation?**

Continuous learning is crucial in leadership and navigation because:

- **Adaptability**: It helps leaders and navigators adapt to the changing business environment.

- **Improvement**: It enables continuous improvement of leadership and navigation skills.

- **Innovation**: It fosters innovation in leadership and navigation practices.

Leadership and navigation are not destinations, but journeys. They require continuous learning, practice, reflection, and improvement. They demand courage to face challenges, resilience to overcome setbacks, and humility to learn from mistakes. They necessitate empathy to understand others, integrity to earn trust, and influence to inspire action.

Relationship Management

Building Effective Relationships

Forging strong relationships serves as the foundation for HR's ability to influence, enable, and partner across all levels of the organization. While HR expertise has value, relationship skills make that knowledge actionable. This chapter shares techniques for cultivating trust, rapport, and connections as an HR professional.

Being Authentically Interested

Show sincere interest in understanding people's perspectives, priorities and challenges. Ask thoughtful questions, listen intently, and acknowledge their experiences without judgement. Caring sincerely energizes collaboration.

Finding Common Ground

Discover shared experiences, passions, or values as common ground. What mutual interests or similarities exist? Recognizing our shared humanity enables trust and eases tensions amidst differences.

Extending Empathy

Demonstrate empathy by imagining yourself in the other's situation given their context and pressures. Express care through body language and validating their emotions. Empathy dissolves defensiveness.

Owning Mistakes

When relationships hit bumps, have the courage to sincerely own mistakes and apologize for any role you played without caveats. Our humanity shows in how we recover.

Speaking Openly But Respectfully

Share your own experiences and needs transparently to enrich understanding. But maintain respect when expressing contrary views. Discuss tough topics with care, not accusations.

Following Through Reliably

Do what you say you will do consistently, even in simple matters. Follow through demonstrates dependability and builds credibility for bigger asks. Don't overcommit.

Extending Trust

Start interactions assuming positive intent in others and trusting their capabilities. But verify outcomes. Beware knee-jerk suspicions while staying attuned to red flags if trust is broken.

Finding Shared Goals

Align on mutual goals and how each person can contribute based on respective strengths. Shared purpose bonded by strengths fosters complementary teamwork.

Being Consistent

While tailoring your style, ensure consistency in upholding organizational values, priorities and standards of professionalism across all interactions regardless of rank. Consistency enables respect.

Staying Generous

Don't keep score in relationships. Avoid grudge holding or tit-for-tat attitudes. Nurture generosity of spirit toward others for the sake of the collective mission.

People change organizations. Rich relationships bridge divides and overcome distrust to enable collaboration. HR sets the tone through compassion, integrity and commitment to understanding. The rest follows.

Conflict Resolution Techniques

Workplace conflict is inevitable, but destructive conflict can shatter teamwork and undermine culture. As relationship stewards, HR professionals must master the art of guiding conflict toward constructive resolutions. This chapter explores techniques for mediating disputes and helping people align on solutions.

Remaining Impartial

Avoid taking sides in a conflict, even if power dynamics are uneven. Stay neutral and impartial so all parties feel heard. Focus on achieving mutual understanding and aim for win-win scenarios.

Letting People Vent First

Allow each person to share their perspective, frustrations and emotions with minimal interruption. Listen attentively and without judgment. Feeling heard de-escalates tension. Validate experiences.

Finding Common Interests

Once emotions cool, pivot to common ground. Identify shared goals, needs or values to unite parties constructively. Mutual interests provide incentive to compromise.

Asking Clarifying Questions

Use probing questions to better understand root causes and unpack complex details. Avoid leading questions. The goal is full clarity for all, not confirming assumptions.

Reframing Positions

Help reframe fixed, opposing positions into shared interests and values. "You want efficient operations, and you want employee wellbeing - how can we achieve both?" This shifts mindsets.

Generating Solutions Together

Move into joint problem-solving mode by having each side suggest constructive solutions while prohibiting personal attacks. Merge the best ideas into shared options.

Discussing Consequences

Explore potential consequences if the conflict remains unresolved, emphasizing impacts to shared goals. Contrast those with how compromise benefits all. Make the path clear.

Being Future-Focused

Detangle conversations stuck rehashing the past by refocusing on wishes moving forward. How can we work together going forward?" Redirect energy into building the future.

Finding Middle Ground

When struggling for mutually agreeable solutions, identify middle ground that provides a partial win for both sides. It may not be perfect, but gets them talking.

Securing Commitment

Once alignment is reached, ensure firm commitment by having parties summarize agreed upon actions and check for acceptance by all. Schedule follow-ups to verify progress.

Unresolved conflicts waste precious energy and destroy trust. With active listening, impartiality and skillful mediation, HR can guide adversaries into shared understanding and collaborative problem solving. That transforms conflict into growth.

Networking and Collaboration in HR

The people-centric nature of HR makes outreach and partnership-building essential skills. By nurturing diverse connections and collaborations across functions, organizations and even industries, HR expands perspectives and delivers greater impact. This chapter provides strategies for networking and alliance-building.

Seeking Cross-Functional Partners

Identify key stakeholders across departments like Finance, Sales, R&D and more whose alignment helps advance HR goals. Get to know their priorities through 1:1s or team meetings. Explore where synergies exist.

Building Camaraderie

Find casual opportunities to foster community and camaraderie with peers company-wide through meetings over coffee, lunches, volunteering, after-work social events etc. The foundation of strong ties often starts informally.

Offering Assistance

Make it known you're eager to support colleagues' efforts when appropriate. Share resources, knowledge, or connections that could benefit them. Adding value fosters reciprocity and goodwill over time.

Following Up

After professional encounters, follow up to share relevant articles, resources, or ideas sparked by the discussion. This demonstrates genuine interest and builds relationships step-by-step.

Joining Committees

Volunteer for cross-functional project teams, wellness initiatives, diversity councils, or other groups that require HR input while enabling collaboration. Bring value through contributions.

Practicing Generosity

Approach networking with a generosity mindset, not transactionality. Give more than you ask for. The broader benefits of sharing knowledge and opportunities outweigh quid pro quo.

Leveraging Social Media

Expand your network and knowledge through professional platforms like LinkedIn. Share articles, comment on trends, and interact. But avoid over-promotion - focus on value.

Attending Conferences

Industry conferences allow networking with fellow HR professionals to exchange ideas, triage challenges, and discover new solutions. Identify relevant national/regional events.

Seeking Mentors

Seasoned mentors expand our perspectives through wisdom and experiences. Respectfully connect with veterans and leaders to learn. Offer your skills to mentor others in return.

Staying Authentic

While shaping your personal brand, remain authentic in all interactions. Pursue connections based on shared interests, not artificial schmoozing. Sincerity shines through.

Partners amplify outcomes. A diverse network shared generously offers new insights and possibilities. By building trust and community, HR accomplishes more.

Stakeholder Management

Organizations depend on strategic HR professionals to build partnerships and influence across a matrix of internal and external stakeholders. Managing diverse stakeholder needs artfully is essential for unlocking support. This chapter explores frameworks, strategies and competencies for effective stakeholder management.

Mapping Stakeholders

Identify all groups and individuals impacted by or invested in HR programs using a Power/Interest Grid. Categorize stakeholders based on their power to influence outcomes and level of interest. Tailor actions accordingly.

Understanding Motivations

Get to know stakeholder groups deeply - their objectives, challenges, concerns, values and biases. This insight enables emphasizing the benefits of shared goals versus solely stating HR's aims.

Crafting Targeted Messaging

Customize communication style, channels, frequency and content appeal based on each stakeholder group. Lean into their priorities and mindsets. A one-size-fits-all approach dilutes impact.

Developing Champions

Cultivate a network of advocates across senior leaders, managers and frontline teams. Equip them with toolkits and resources to amplify HR messages within their spheres of influence.

Providing Value

Offer HR knowledge, services, data, tools and support that directly help stakeholders further their goals. Shared value strengthens partnerships and credibility for stakeholder buy-in.

Collaborating Closely

Involve high power/interest groups actively in solution design through co-creation sessions, advisory committees, prototyping, pilot projects and open communication channels. Make their voices heard.

Overcommunicating

Err on the side of overcommunicating with stakeholders through multiple platforms and channels. Convey key messages repeatedly, transparently and clearly. Leave no room for ambiguity or ignorance.

Managing Up Strategically

Influence senior leaders effectively by learning their priorities, framing HR aims in relation to goals, and mastering executive-facing communication styles. Quantify the value-add.

Addressing Concerns

When resistance arises, listen empathetically to objections and fears. Provide evidence addressing concerns, involve stakeholders in solution-building, and highlight shared interests.

Monitoring Relationships

Check-in regularly at individual and group levels to assess the health of key partnerships. Are stakeholders satisfied? What could improve? Nurture lasting alliances.

By balancing strategy and empathy, HR strengthens critical bonds across the organization to amplify programs, scale innovation, and build a culture of partnership.

Practice Questions and Detailed Answers

Relationship management is a crucial skill in both personal and professional life. It involves nurturing and maintaining positive relationships with others. Let's explore this topic further with a set of practice questions and detailed answers.

1. **What is relationship management?**

Relationship management is the process of building, maintaining, and enhancing positive relationships with others, including customers, employees, partners, and stakeholders. It involves understanding others' needs and expectations, communicating effectively, resolving conflicts, and collaborating for mutual benefit.

2. **Why is relationship management important?**

The importance of relationship management lies in its ability to:

- **Collaboration**: Enhance collaboration and teamwork.
- **Trust**: Build and sustain trust and goodwill.
- **Conflict Resolution**: Facilitate effective conflict resolution.
- **Customer Retention**: Enhance customer satisfaction and retention.
- **Business Success**: Contribute to business success and sustainability.

3. **What are some key skills in relationship management?**

Key skills in relationship management include:

- **Active Listening**: Listening to understand others' perspectives.
- **Empathy**: Understanding and resonating with others' feelings.
- **Communication**: Communicating effectively and respectfully.

63

- **Conflict Resolution**: Resolving conflicts in a constructive manner.

- **Collaboration**: Collaborating effectively with others.

4. **How can one develop relationship management skills?**

Developing relationship management skills involves:

- **Learning**: Understanding the principles and techniques of relationship management.

- **Practice**: Applying these principles and techniques in real-life scenarios.

- **Feedback**: Seeking and acting upon feedback from others.

- **Reflection**: Reflecting on one's interactions and their outcomes.

- **Continuous Improvement**: Continuously learning and improving.

5. **What role does empathy play in relationship management?**

Empathy plays a crucial role in relationship management. It helps to:

- **Understand**: Understand others' feelings and perspectives.

- **Connect**: Connect with others on a deeper level.

- **Trust**: Build trust and goodwill.

- **Resolve Conflicts**: Resolve conflicts in a more understanding and respectful manner.

6. **How can organizations support relationship management?**

Organizations can support relationship management by:

- **Training**: Providing training and development opportunities.

- **Culture**: Creating a culture that values relationship management.

- **Tools**: Providing tools and resources for relationship management.

- **Recognition**: Recognizing and rewarding good relationship management.

7. **What is the relationship between relationship management and customer satisfaction?**

Relationship management contributes to customer satisfaction by:

- **Understanding**: Understanding customers' needs and expectations.

- **Communication**: Communicating effectively with customers.

- **Service**: Providing excellent service to customers.
- **Trust**: Building and maintaining trust with customers.

8. **How can relationship management contribute to conflict resolution?**

Relationship management contributes to conflict resolution by:

- **Understanding**: Understanding the sources of conflict and the perspectives of conflicting parties.
- **Communication**: Facilitating open and respectful communication.
- **Mediation**: Mediating between conflicting parties to find a mutually acceptable solution.
- **Reconciliation**: Helping conflicting parties reconcile and maintain their relationship.

9. **What are some challenges in relationship management and how can they be addressed?**

Challenges in relationship management can include misunderstandings, conflicts, and lack of trust. These can be addressed by:

- **Misunderstandings**: Improving communication to prevent and address misunderstandings.
- **Conflicts**: Developing conflict resolution skills to manage conflicts effectively.
- **Lack of Trust**: Building trust through honesty, reliability, and transparency.

10. **How can relationship management enhance team performance?**

Relationship management enhances team performance by:

- **Collaboration**: Facilitating effective collaboration among team members.
- **Motivation**: Building positive relationships that motivate team members.
- **Conflict Resolution**: Resolving conflicts that can disrupt team performance.
- **Trust**: Building trust within the team.

Relationship management is a journey of understanding, connection, and collaboration. It involves understanding others' perspectives, connecting with them on a deeper level, and collaborating for mutual benefit. It requires active listening, effective communication, empathy, and conflict resolution.

Talent Acquisition and Retention

Recruitment Strategies

Attracting top talent is pivotal to organization success, making strategic recruiting a priority for HR professionals. Beyond basic practices, proactive and innovative recruiting builds competitive advantage through targeted outreach, employment branding, and candidate experience. This chapter explores techniques to optimize recruiting capabilities.

Modernizing Job Descriptions

Take traditional job descriptions beyond duties by incorporating company culture, total rewards, employee value proposition and growth opportunities. This expands appeal.

Promoting Referrals

Referral programs that reward employees for high-quality candidate recommendations are a proven cost-effective source. Make referral simple and highlight at onboarding.

Maximizing Social Recruiting

Promote open roles across multiple social platforms using engaging content like videos or employee testimonials. Monitor analytics to refine messaging and outreach.

Optimizing Career Sites

Ensure career pages communicate your value proposition, showcase culture, and explain application processes clearly. Feature diverse employee stories. Enable mobile apply.

Building Talent Pipelines

Get ahead of hiring demands by continuously cultivating relationships with prospective candidates. Keep talent pools warm through networking events and engagement.

Automating Screening

Leverage automation tools and AI to pre-screen applicants consistently against required qualifications, enabling recruiters to focus on culture and skill assessment.

Conducting Skills Assessments

Incorporate customized skills assessments like problem-solving scenarios, simulations, writing samples or videos to evaluate competencies beyond resumes. Assess potential.

Streamlining Hiring Workflows

Remove delays and excess touchpoints in requisition approvals, feedback loops, and offer letter delivery through Lean process improvement techniques.

Branding the Candidate Experience

Make a great impression through regular communication, providing expectations, thoughtful interview design, timely follow up, and expressing appreciation even to rejects.

Analyzing Metrics

Track and analyze recruiting metrics like cost per hire, time to fill, source percentages and offer acceptance rates. Review against benchmarks to guide strategy.

Progressive recruiting transforms hiring into a competitive advantage through data, branding, automation and process excellence. By improving how talent is attracted and selected, HR enables organizational success.

Selection Processes and Techniques

Hiring top talent requires structured, unbiased selection processes that thoroughly assess candidates. HR professionals must employ techniques to screen applicants consistently and design insightful interviews revealing skills, mindsets and cultural fit. This chapter explores proven selection approaches.

Defining Job Success Factors

Clarify must-have qualifications, specialized competencies, and soft skills that drive excellence in the role through job analysis techniques. Use this profile to craft screening criteria.

Screening Objectively

Avoid unconscious bias by anonymizing applications and using scorecards to rate experience, skills and qualifications systematically. Consider skills testing.

Structuring Interviews Thoughtfully

Design interviews that blend behavioral, situational and culture-add questions aligned to success factors. Ask for examples and problem solving. Standardize questions asked across candidates.

Building a Diverse Panel

Involve a cross-functional panel with diverse perspectives in interviews. Panelists can assess different aspects of capability. Promote inclusion.

Probing Past Experiences

Explore track records of achievements, critical thinking, teamwork, overcoming challenges and leadership to understand candidates' natural strengths and motivations. Spotlights growth potential.

Assessing Cultural Fit

Look for value and priority alignment around important cultural traits like teamwork, innovation, ethics, diversity, and service. Protect against culture-add alone.

Enabling 2-Way Dialogue

Allow ample reciprocal discussion time for candidates to assess role fit, understand priorities and build rapport. Answering their questions also provides insights.

Checking References Deeply

Seek detailed input from provided references on responsibilities, work quality, strengths, development areas, and team interactions to verify past performance and conduct.

Avoiding Bias Traps

Recognize common types of bias like snap judgments, negative weighting of gaps, irrelevant personal preferences and inconsistent criteria. Focus evaluations on outlined success factors.

Selling the Role

Make candidates want to accept offers by sharing compelling visions, culture benefits, growth paths and passion for the work. Enable informed decisions.

Rigorous, unbiased selection processes allow HR teams to deeply understand candidate potential, skills and motivations for strongest role fit and performance. Structure is essential to hiring excellence.

Employee Onboarding and Socialization

Onboarding presents a pivotal first impression of the employee experience. Thoughtful onboarding and socialization enables new hires to become productive and engaged at speed. This chapter explores best practices in orientation, training, cultural immersion and ongoing ramp-up support.

Planning Comprehensive Programs

Well-designed onboarding involves much more than forms and handbooks. Map detailed curriculums spanning pre-boarding outreach to 90-day plans including milestones, resources, and program owners.

Making Early Connections

Have managers introduce themselves by phone or video before start dates. Assign peer buddies to navigate social nuances and make personal connections. Enable networking.

Overcommunicating Logistics

Provide extensive logistical details on locations, attire, parking, technology setup, contacts and scheduling to reduce first-day anxieties. Make expectations crystal clear.

Offering Inspiring Orientations

Focus day one on inspiring company purpose, values, strategy and goals through dynamic presentations from leadership, stories, and interactive sessions rather than just policies.

Immersing in Culture

Share company history, traditions, cultural tenets, inside lingo, organizational structure and unwritten rules of behavior to help new hires adopt cultural mindsets quickly.

Cross-Training Peers

rotations where new team members shadow and learn from peers in complementary roles builds network and big picture understanding. Prevent knowledge silos.

Assigning Bite-Sized Projects

Ramp productivity through a series of small, achievable onboarding assignments allowing quick wins. Provide ample support and celebrate successes.

Checking-In Regularly

Managers should connect at least weekly in the first months to discuss progress, answer questions, and proactively address any needs. Make new hires feel cared for.

Measuring Onboarding ROI

Evaluate programs through new hire surveys, retention data, manager feedback and metrics like ramp-up time and performance. Identify improvement opportunities.

Sustaining Support Networks

Facilitate ongoing peer cohorts for mutual learning and troubleshooting as employees continue mastering skills after formal onboarding ends. Community aids retention.

When executed strategically, onboarding transforms scattered employment tasks into cohesive experiences that engage, develop and retain top talent from day one. HR lays the foundation for impact.

Retention Strategies

Attracting talent provides little value if top performers consistently leave. HR professionals must prioritize proactive retention through fostering engagement, growth, inclusion, wellbeing and rewards to sustain a thriving workforce. This chapter explores techniques to retain and empower talent.

Measuring Sentiment

Regular employee surveys, interviews and focus groups provide vital retention insights around satisfaction, burnout risks, equity concerns and desired improvements. Track trends over time.

Strengthening Managers

Equip managers to support their teams through training on motivational techniques, personalized development, flexible leadership, constructive feedback delivery, work-life balance and signs someone is disengaging.

Building Community

Facilitate connections and camaraderie through colleague introductions, mentoring programs, employee resource groups, social events and community service activities. Human ties retain.

Offering Development

Provide clear growth pathways and developmental opportunities like lateral moves, stretch assignments, tuition assistance, mentorships and training. Help people continuously expand skills.

Enabling Voice

Create open forums for employees at all levels to share ideas, questions and concerns without fear. Make people feel genuinely heard and close feedback loops.

Promoting Work-Life Balance

Guard against burnout with policies supporting healthy work hours, paid time off, remote work flexibility, caregiver leave, sabbaticals and mental health. Model balance at the top.

Analyzing Exit Data

Review exit interview themes, turnover costs and analytics to pinpoint risk factors for leaving. Diagnose where stronger retention efforts are needed.

Targeting Rewards

Beyond compensation and benefits, leverage personalized rewards like public awards, gift cards, extra time off, choice assignments and handwritten notes of appreciation.

Checking In

Proactively check in on newer hires within the first 6 months and employees in high churn roles. Reconnect people to purpose and community.

Staying Vigilant

Continuously evaluate policies, projects and culture against a retention lens. Are people valued, included, supported and heard? Any retention gaps require swift action.

With care and commitment to understanding employee needs, HR enables sustainable success through nurturing an engaged, invested workforce where people feel empowered to stay and thrive.

Practice Questions and Detailed Answers

Talent acquisition and retention are at the heart of any successful organization. It's a process aimed at attracting, hiring, and retaining employees who possess the required skills and potential for the organization. This chapter presents you with ten practice questions and detailed answers about this critical aspect of human resources management.

1. **What is talent acquisition?**

Talent acquisition refers to the process of identifying, attracting, and acquiring skilled individuals to meet the organization's strategic and operational needs. It involves succession planning, employer branding, recruitment, interviewing, selection, and onboarding.

2. **What are some strategies for effective talent acquisition?**

Effective talent acquisition strategies include:

- **Employer Branding**: Enhance your organization's reputation to attract top talent.

- **Candidate Experience**: Streamline the recruitment process to improve candidate experience.

- **Diversity and Inclusion**: Implement diversity and inclusion initiatives to attract a broad range of candidates.

- **Technology**: Leverage recruitment technologies to identify and attract potential candidates.

- **Data-driven Decisions**: Use data analytics to inform talent acquisition strategies.

3. **What is talent retention?**

Talent retention refers to strategies and practices organizations employ to prevent valuable employees from leaving their jobs. It involves creating an appealing work culture, competitive compensation, opportunities for career progression, and maintaining a work-life balance.

4. **What are some strategies for effective talent retention?**

Effective talent retention strategies include:

- **Career Development**: Provide opportunities for career advancement and skills enhancement.

- **Recognition**: Recognize and reward employees' efforts and achievements.

- **Work Environment**: Foster a positive, inclusive, and supportive work culture.

- **Competitive Compensation**: Offer competitive salaries, benefits, and non-monetary rewards.

- **Engagement**: Encourage employee participation in decision-making processes.

5. **How does talent acquisition influence an organization's success?**

Talent acquisition directly impacts an organization's success by:

- **Performance**: Acquiring the right talent can enhance the organization's performance.

- **Culture**: Bringing diverse individuals can foster innovation and enrich the organizational culture.

- **Growth**: Hiring individuals with the right skills can drive the organization's growth and competitive advantage.

- **Retention**: A well-planned talent acquisition strategy can improve employee retention.

6. **What is the relationship between talent acquisition and retention?**

Talent acquisition and retention are two sides of the same coin. While talent acquisition focuses on bringing the right individuals into the organization, retention ensures they remain engaged and committed to their roles. A balanced approach to both can lead to a high-performing, diverse, and loyal workforce.

7. **What role does employer branding play in talent acquisition and retention?**

Employer branding plays a significant role in both talent acquisition and retention. A strong employer brand can attract high-quality candidates and can also make current employees prouder and more likely to stay with the organization.

8. How can data analytics support talent acquisition and retention?

Data analytics can support talent acquisition and retention by:

- **Insights**: Providing insights into the labor market, candidate preferences, and employee behavior.

- **Decision Making**: Informing decision-making in recruitment, selection, and retention strategies.

- **Performance**: Measuring the effectiveness of talent acquisition and retention strategies.

- **Predictive Analysis**: Predicting future hiring needs and potential employee turnover.

9. What are some challenges in talent acquisition and retention?

Some common challenges in talent acquisition and retention include:

- **Attracting Talent**: Finding and attracting the right candidates in a competitive job market.

- **Employee Engagement**: Keeping employees engaged and committed to their roles.

- **Diversity**: Attracting and retaining a diverse workforce.

- **Turnover**: Preventing high-performing employees from leaving the organization.

These challenges can be addressed by developing a strong employer brand, creating an inclusive culture, offering competitive compensation, and using data analytics.

10. How can organizations ensure continuous improvement in talent acquisition and retention?

Organizations can ensure continuous improvement in talent acquisition and retention by:

- **Feedback**: Regularly seeking and acting upon feedback from candidates and employees.

- **Monitoring**: Regularly monitoring the effectiveness of talent acquisition and retention strategies.

- **Learning**: Learning from best practices in the industry.

- **Innovation**: Continuously innovating and adapting to changes in the labor market and workforce demographics.

HR Strategic Planning

The Role of HR in Strategic Planning

The Human Resources (HR) department plays a significant role in strategic planning. By acting as a bridge between the organization's strategy and its human capital, HR can help shape the organization's future. This chapter delves into the crucial role HR plays in strategic planning, offering practical advice and insights for beginners.

Understanding Strategic Planning

Strategic planning refers to the process an organization undergoes to define its direction and make decisions on resource allocation, including its capital and people, to pursue this strategy. It involves setting long-term goals, determining the best approach to achieve those goals, and aligning various parts of the organization to support that direction.

The Role of HR in Strategic Planning

Traditionally, HR's role was administrative, focusing on hiring, compensation, employee relations, and compliance. However, the HR function has evolved, and it now plays a strategic role in organizations. HR's influence stretches to strategic planning, where it can contribute by:

- **Aligning HR Strategy with Business Strategy:** HR professionals must understand the organization's strategic plan to develop and implement an HR strategy that supports it. This could involve talent management, succession planning, workforce planning, and employee development initiatives that align with the organization's goals.

- **Talent Acquisition and Management:** HR plays a critical role in acquiring and managing talent that aligns with the organization's strategic goals. This includes identifying the skills and competencies the organization will need in the future, sourcing candidates who meet these requirements, and implementing programs to develop and retain these employees.

- **Succession Planning:** HR oversees the succession planning process, which involves identifying and developing potential leaders within the organization. Succession planning ensures the organization has the leadership it needs to execute its strategy, even in the event of unforeseen changes.

- **Change Management:** When the strategic plan involves significant changes, HR plays a key role in managing this change. This can involve communication strategies, training programs, and other initiatives to help employees understand and adapt to the changes.

- **Measuring and Improving Employee Performance:** HR implements performance management systems to measure and improve employee performance. By aligning these systems with the organization's strategic goals, HR can help ensure employees' efforts contribute to these goals.

- **Cultivating Organizational Culture:** HR helps shape the organization's culture, which can significantly impact its ability to achieve its strategic goals. A positive, inclusive culture can improve employee performance, innovation, and collaboration.

HR's Strategic Partnering with Other Departments

To effectively contribute to strategic planning, HR must partner with other departments. By understanding the challenges and opportunities facing these departments, HR can better align its initiatives with the organization's overall strategy. This involves regular communication and collaboration with department leaders to understand their needs and provide support.

Enhancing HR's Strategic Role

To enhance HR's strategic role, HR professionals should:

- Develop business acumen: Understanding the organization's industry, competitors, and customers can help HR make more strategic decisions.

- Improve analytics skills: HR analytics can provide valuable insights for strategic planning, such as predicting future workforce needs or identifying patterns in employee turnover.

- Foster relationships: Building relationships with leaders across the organization can position HR as a trusted advisor in strategic planning.

- Advocate for employees: HR can represent employees' perspectives in strategic planning, ensuring their needs and ideas are considered.

HR's role in strategic planning is crucial, and it's more than just a function of the organization. It's a strategic partner, contributing to the direction and success of the company. By aligning HR initiatives with the organization's strategy, HR can help create a workforce that's engaged, productive, and ready to carry out the organization's mission.

Aligning HR Strategy with Business Goals

For HR to enable organizational success, talent priorities must directly support overarching business objectives. Strategic alignment requires understanding the broader corporate strategy and repositioning HR initiatives to advance critical goals. This chapter explores integrating HR efforts seamlessly with business imperatives.

Clarifying Corporate Strategy

First, comprehend the core elements of the business strategy - target growth, cost leadership, innovation, customer experience etc. Understand upcoming strategic projects and how they intend to achieve aims.

Identifying HR Implications

Analyze strategy implications for workforce needs, capabilities, structures, and culture. What people, skills, behaviors and systems will strategic changes require long-term? Spot gaps.

Prioritizing HR Programs

Evaluate all HR programs through a strategy lens. Which most accelerate strategic capabilities and performance versus just maintaining operations? Refocus efforts on initiatives fueling strategy.

Developing Strategic Workforce Plans

Forecast talent needs under strategic scenarios using data on demographics, turnover, retirement eligibility and more. Outline sourcing plans, costs, and timelines to meet demands.

Building Critical Capabilities

Strengthen competencies like new technology expertise, product innovation, customer-centricity and analytics that enable strategic differentiation through targeted recruiting, development programs, and training.

Restructuring for Agility

Evaluate organizational structures, decision-making authority, cross-functional processes and teams against strategic agility needs. Are changes required to empower faster reaction?

Championing Cultural Evolution

Determine desired cultural traits like risk-taking, collaboration, efficiency and examine misalignments with strategic aims. Guide cultural evolution through leadership messaging and modeled behaviors.

Tying Performance to Strategy

Link workforce and leadership performance metrics to strategic target achievement, not just activity. Evaluate individuals on how their efforts collectively advance strategic results.

Advising Executives

Serve as talent advisors to senior leaders on strategy-driven org design, change management, talent implications of M&A and strategic trade-offs like speed vs. risk.

Updating Reward Systems

Incentivize behaviors that support strategy like innovation, customer focus, and collaboration through compensation programs, promotions, awards, and perks. Link rewards visibly to strategy.

An HR strategy embedded within wider business goals enables people programs to directly activate organizational performance and competitive advantage. Strategy-driven talent leadership is truly transformative.

Workforce Planning and Employment

Workforce planning is a systematic, fully integrated organizational process that involves proactively planning ahead to avoid talent surpluses or shortages. It is based on the premise that an organization can be staffed more efficiently if it forecasts its talent needs as well as the actual supply of talent that is or will be available.

Understanding Workforce Planning

Workforce planning is a continual process used to align the needs and priorities of the organization with those of its workforce to ensure it can meet its legislative, regulatory, service and production requirements and organizational objectives. It helps identify the workforce implications, current and future, of the business strategy and provides evidence for investing in people.

The Connection between Workforce Planning and Employment

The process of workforce planning includes analyzing current workforce, determining future workforce needs, identifying the gap between the present and the future, and implementing solutions so the organization can accomplish its mission, goals, and strategic plan.

Employment is a relationship between two parties, usually based on contract where work is paid for, where one party, which may be a corporation, for profit, not-for-profit organization, co-operative or other entity is the employer and the other is the employee.

Workforce planning, then, is the strategic alignment of an organization's human capital with its business direction. It is a methodical process of analyzing the current workforce, identifying future workforce needs, and implementing solutions to close the talent gap.

Steps in Workforce Planning

Workforce planning can be broken down into a few key steps:

1. **Environmental Scan:** This involves analysing both external and internal trends and factors that may affect the workforce.

2. **Current Workforce Profile:** This is a comprehensive understanding of the organization's current workforce profile.

3. **Future Workforce View:** Determining the organization's future staffing needs based on its strategic goals.

4. **Gap Analysis:** Identifying the gaps between the current workforce and future needs.

5. **Solution Analysis:** Developing and implementing strategies to close the gaps.

The Role of HR in Workforce Planning

The HR team plays a crucial role in workforce planning. They are responsible for coordinating the process, facilitating discussions about the workforce, and providing data and analysis to support decision making. HR's role in workforce planning can be broken down into four main areas:

- **Data Collection and Analysis:** HR collects and analyzes data on a range of workforce metrics, such as turnover rates, employee satisfaction, and the time it takes to fill vacancies.

- **Workforce Strategy Development:** Based on the data and analysis, HR develops a workforce strategy that aligns with the organization's strategic goals.

- **Implementation:** HR is responsible for implementing the workforce strategy. This could involve a range of activities, such as recruiting new staff, developing talent management programs, or improving employee retention.

- **Monitoring and Evaluation:** HR monitors the workforce and evaluates the effectiveness of the workforce strategy. They adjust the strategy as needed based on this ongoing evaluation.

Workforce Planning Challenges and Solutions

While workforce planning is critical, it can also be challenging. Some common challenges include changing demographic trends, shifts in the economy, technological advancements, and changes in the industry or competitive landscape. Despite these challenges, an effective workforce planning process can help an organization mitigate risks, make informed decisions, and achieve its strategic goals.

Implementing a robust workforce planning process requires commitment from leadership, a clear understanding of the organization's strategic goals, and effective data analysis. Technology can also aid in this process, with various software and tools available to assist in data collection, analysis, and strategy development.

Succession Planning

With today's aging workforce, organizations must proactively prepare leaders for critical roles through robust succession planning programs. Beyond mere replacement planning, strategic succession builds bench strength, accelerates development, and sustains a healthy talent pipeline. This chapter provides guidance on succession best practices.

Defining Business Critical Roles

Conduct workforce analyses using metrics like turnover risk, projected growth, and strategic impact to identify roles absolutely vital to maintain. Focus initial succession efforts here.

Assessing Capabilities

Compare incumbent capabilities against role requirements to determine Skill gaps successors must fill through mentoring, job rotations, training and stretch assignments. Develop to needs.

Casting a Wide Net

Avoid early successor identification or only considering incumbents for development. Market and recruit externally to expand the pool. Seek nontraditional but high potential candidates.

Using Assessments Strategically

Leverage 180/360 assessments, personality tests, values inventories, skills simulations and cognitive tests to evaluate leadership potential from all angles. Assess derailers too.

Democratizing Through Transparency

Communicate succession processes and criteria openly enterprise-wide. Make programs equitable and accessible to all. Transparency fuels engagement.

Providing Exposure

Expose high potential employees to senior leaders through committees, projects, networking events and speaker forums. Increase visibility of emerging talent.

Offering Stretch Opportunities

Develop leadership muscles with short-term developmental assignments like committee leadership, special projects, interim manager roles and task force positions. Practice real-world application.

Formalizing Development Plans

Document concrete IDP's outlining skill development goals, on-the-job learning, mentors, and formal training needed to address development gaps identified through assessments.

Evaluating Readiness

Use readiness criteria like expertise levels, feedback, program completion, and situational leadership tests to determine if successors are prepared for promotion when vacancies arise. Wait for readiness.

Monitoring Engagement

Prevent flight risk of passed-over candidates by providing transparency on development status, creating individualized growth paths, and offering guidance. Keep talent engaged.

Strategic succession planning sustains leadership continuity, spurs development, and promotes inclusion by proactively preparing emerging talent through rigorous assessment and growth experiences.

Practice Questions and Detailed Answers

HR strategic planning goes beyond hiring and firing; it's about aligning human capital with the organization's overall strategic objectives. The purpose of this chapter is to delve into ten practice questions and provide comprehensive answers that will help you understand HR strategic planning better.

1. **What is HR strategic planning?**

HR strategic planning is the process of aligning the human resource strategy with the organization's overall strategic goals. It involves identifying workforce needs, developing talent, fostering a conducive work environment, and implementing HR initiatives that support the organization's objectives.

2. **Why is HR strategic planning important?**

HR strategic planning is crucial because:

- It helps to ensure that the organization has the right people with the right skills to execute its strategy.

- It aids in the anticipation of future workforce needs.

- It fosters engagement by aligning individual goals with organizational ones.

- It helps the organization stay competitive in attracting and retaining top talent.

3. **What are the key steps in HR strategic planning?**

Key steps in HR strategic planning include:

- Understanding the organization's strategic objectives.

- Conducting a workforce analysis to identify current and future human resource needs.

- Developing HR initiatives and programs to support the organization's strategy.

- Implementing the HR strategy.

- Monitoring and adjusting the strategy as needed.

4. What is a SWOT analysis in HR strategic planning?

A SWOT analysis is a strategic planning tool used to identify an organization's Strengths, Weaknesses, Opportunities, and Threats related to workforce management. This analysis aids in determining the internal and external factors that can impact the organization's ability to meet its strategic objectives.

5. How does workforce analysis contribute to HR strategic planning?

Workforce analysis contributes to HR strategic planning by:

- Providing insights into the current workforce's skills, competencies, and demographics.

- Helping to identify gaps in skills or personnel.

- Assisting in forecasting future workforce needs based on strategic objectives.

- Guiding talent management strategies such as recruitment, retention, and development.

6. What role does talent management play in HR strategic planning?

Talent management plays a critical role in HR strategic planning as it ensures the organization has the right people in the right roles at the right time. It involves talent acquisition, development, retention, and succession planning. Effective talent management supports strategic objectives by ensuring a constant supply of skilled and engaged personnel.

7. How does HR strategic planning support diversity and inclusion?

HR strategic planning can support diversity and inclusion by:

- Identifying diversity and inclusion as strategic objectives.

- Implementing recruitment and retention strategies that foster a diverse workforce.

- Creating initiatives to promote an inclusive culture.

- Monitoring and adjusting strategies to ensure diversity and inclusion goals are met.

8. **How is HR strategic planning linked to organizational performance?**

HR strategic planning is linked to organizational performance by ensuring that the human resources are in place to execute the organization's strategy effectively. It aids in enhancing productivity, fostering innovation, improving employee satisfaction, and ultimately, driving business performance.

9. **What challenges can arise in HR strategic planning?**

Challenges in HR strategic planning can include:

- Changing workforce demographics and expectations.
- Rapid technological advancements affecting work processes.
- Difficulties in accurately forecasting future workforce needs.
- Resistance to change within the organization.

Strategies to overcome these challenges include staying abreast of workforce trends, leveraging HR technologies, involving stakeholders in the planning process, and fostering a culture of change and learning.

10. **How can HR metrics contribute to HR strategic planning?**

HR metrics can contribute to HR strategic planning by providing data-driven insights into HR processes and outcomes. Metrics such as turnover rate, time to fill, employee engagement scores, and others, can inform the effectiveness of HR strategies and guide adjustments as needed.

Structure of the HR Function

Organizational Structures and HR

An organization's structure profoundly shapes workforce strategy and talent priorities. HR professionals must comprehend structural dynamics, alignments and misalignments to optimize policies and practices for the design. This chapter examines structuring choices and considerations for HR.

Assessing Centralization

Centralized structures consolidate power and decision making at the top while decentralized models distribute authority across business units or geographies. Evaluate cultural readiness and standardization needs.

Enabling Flexibility

More agile structures like matrices, teams, and networks trade some efficiency for greater flexibility, collaboration and innovation. Determine strategic priorities and change pace.

Optimizing Span of Control

Wider managerial spans of control enable leaner cost structures but reduce support for direct reports. Narrower spans foster relationships but limit scalability. Balance trade-offs.

Clarifying Authority

Ambiguous authority breeds conflict and gridlock. Clearly define decision rights and accountabilities across business units, functions and ranks. Avoid power struggles.

Streamlining Hierarchies

Flatter structures remove unnecessary layers that stifle information sharing and agility. But hierarchies provide stability. Right-size based on strategy and culture.

Facilitating Collaboration

Loosen rigid silos with structures that connect people across previously disconnected units through cross-functional teams, committees, and matrix networks. Break down barriers.

Realigning HR

Examine how HR team alignment maps to the organizational blueprint. Adjust to develop specialized expertise for key functions/units, shared services for synergies and Centers of Excellence.

Tailoring Talent Programs

Customize talent initiatives to fit the distinct needs, preferences and challenges of unique business units or satellite locations within the structure. Recognize lack of one-size-fits-all.

Clarifying Career Paths

With matrix and team-based structures, career growth can become ambiguous. Develop clear cross-functional advancement options and project-based leadership roles.

Simplifying Policies

Consolidate and simplify complex, conflicting HR policies and procedures stemming from outdated structural silos or mergers. Lead cultural integration.

HR serves as an architect and aligner to build people strategies fitting the organization's structure. The right human capital approach unlocks efficiencies and adaptability.

HR Service Delivery Models

Human Resources (HR) plays a pivotal role in managing the most valuable asset of an organization: its people. As businesses evolve, so too do the methods and models of delivering HR services. The choice of HR service delivery model can significantly impact an organization's efficiency, cost-effectiveness, and overall employee experience.

Understanding HR Service Delivery Models

An HR service delivery model refers to the framework or system used by HR to provide services to employees. These services can range from recruitment and onboarding to performance management, training, payroll, and benefits administration. The choice of model depends on various factors, including the size of the organization, the nature of its work, its strategic goals, and its available resources.

Types of HR Service Delivery Models

There are several commonly used HR service delivery models, each with its advantages and drawbacks. Let's explore three primary models.

1. **Shared Service Model:** In a shared service model, routine HR tasks are centralized in a shared service center. This model increases efficiency and consistency, reduces costs, and allows HR professionals to focus on strategic tasks. However, it might not cater to the unique needs of individual business units or locations.

2. **Center of Excellence (CoE) Model:** In the CoE model, specialized HR functions are grouped together into 'centers of excellence.' Each CoE focuses on a specific area of HR, such as talent management or learning and development, becoming a hub of expertise and best practices. While this model promotes deep expertise, it may also lead to silos within HR.

3. **Business Partner Model:** The business partner model involves HR professionals working closely with business leaders to develop and implement HR solutions that meet the strategic needs of the business. This model can lead to more strategic HR, but it also requires HR professionals with strong business acumen and the ability to work collaboratively with leaders.

Selecting the Right HR Service Delivery Model

Choosing the right HR service delivery model requires a careful analysis of the organization's needs and goals. Here are a few considerations:

- **Organizational Size and Structure:** Larger organizations with multiple locations may benefit from a shared service model, while smaller, centralized organizations could prefer the business partner model.

- **Business Strategy:** If the business strategy involves significant change or innovation, the business partner or CoE model may be most appropriate.

- **HR Capability:** The organization's HR capability, including the skills and expertise of its HR team, will also influence the choice of model.

- **Technology:** The availability and sophistication of HR technology can also impact the choice of service delivery model.

Implementing an HR Service Delivery Model

Implementing a new HR service delivery model is a significant change initiative that requires careful planning and management. It may involve restructuring the HR team, changing HR processes, and implementing new HR technology.

Change management is crucial during this process to ensure that all stakeholders understand the reasons for the change, the benefits of the new model, and their role in implementing it. Regular communication, training, and support will help to ensure a smooth transition.

Evaluating the Effectiveness of an HR Service Delivery Model

Once the new HR service delivery model is implemented, it's important to regularly evaluate its effectiveness. This evaluation can be based on a range of metrics, including cost-effectiveness, efficiency, service quality, and stakeholder satisfaction. Feedback from end-users, including employees and managers, can also provide valuable insights.

Remember, there's no one-size-fits-all HR service delivery model. The best model for your organization depends on your specific context and needs. And as your organization evolves, your HR service delivery model may need to evolve too.

Role of HR in Mergers and Acquisitions

Mergers and acquisitions represent major organizational transitions requiring deft leadership to unite cultures, systems and workforces. HR plays an integral role in due diligence, integration planning, and nurturing engagement through uncertainty. This chapter outlines key strategies for guiding combinations.

Assessing Cultural Alignment

Analyze cultural compatibility regarding values, work styles, norms and talent priorities upfront. Misaligned cultures heighten integration challenges and employee flight risks. Flag potential pitfalls.

Evaluating HR Systems

Thoroughly compare compensation models, performance management, HRIS systems, policies and programs. Determine gaps and required investments to transition or consolidate platforms.

Leading Due Diligence

Partner with executives to conduct workforce due diligence on talent demographics, retention risks, labor relations, and compensation competitiveness. Identify liabilities.

Modeling Organizational Designs

Propose new organizational charts and structures to capture synergies across merged teams. Balance continuity with change. Outline decision authorities and accountabilities.

Building an Integration Plan

Define a detailed post-merger integration roadmap and timeline addressing priorities like executive alignment, system transitions, retention strategies, and change management milestones.

Preserving Culture Essentials

Determine cultural elements, like customer service values, worth preserving from each organization. Develop ways to unite cultures by celebrating shared strengths.

Preparing Leadership

Train leaders on guiding teams through transition, maintaining morale, addressing concerns, and modeling desired behaviors. Equip them to answer tough talent questions.

Driving Change Management

Proactively support employees through robust communications, culture-building events, individualized outplacement services, and change networking groups. Maintain productivity amidst uncertainty.

Realigning Talent

Evaluate redundancies objectively but remain empathetic. Handle layoffs respectfully per policies. Assess new talent needs under combined business models.

Tracking Integration Progress

Establish metrics on milestones, productivity, turnover, and ongoing culture health. Analyze integration successes and pain points. Refine approach.

With strategic foresight, compassion and unwavering commitment to people, HR enables organizations to emerge stronger from disruptive combinations. We unite, transition and inspire.

Practice Questions and Detailed Answers

The structure of the Human Resources (HR) function is a key aspect of organizational design that directly impacts its ability to deliver on strategic objectives. This chapter will guide you through ten practical questions about the structure of the HR function, providing you with detailed answers and actionable insights.

1. **What is the Structure of the HR Function?**

The structure of the HR function refers to the arrangement of roles, responsibilities, and relationships within the HR department. It involves determining how HR tasks are divided and coordinated, and who reports to whom. This can vary greatly depending on the size, industry, and strategic objectives of the organization.

2. **Why is the Structure of the HR Function Important?**

The structure of the HR function is crucial because:

- It defines roles and responsibilities, reducing confusion and enhancing focus.

- It impacts the efficiency and effectiveness of HR operations.

- It influences HR's ability to align with and support strategic objectives.

- It can affect the HR team's morale and productivity.

3. **What Factors Influence the Structure of the HR Function?**

Factors that influence the structure of the HR function include:

- The size of the organization: Larger organizations typically have more specialized HR roles.

- The industry: Certain industries may require specialized HR expertise.

- The strategic objectives of the organization: HR structure should align with and support these objectives.

- Regulatory requirements: These may necessitate specific roles or responsibilities.

4. **What are the Common Models for HR Structure?**

Common models for HR structure include:

- Functional: HR is divided into specialized roles such as recruitment, training, and benefits.

- Shared services: HR tasks are centralized into a shared service center, often with self-service options for employees.

- Business partner: HR professionals are embedded into business units to provide strategic support.

- Matrix: Combines elements of the above models to fit the unique needs of the organization.

5. **How Does the Structure of the HR Function Impact Its Effectiveness?**

The structure of the HR function can greatly impact its effectiveness. An optimal structure allows HR to deliver services efficiently, respond to issues promptly, and provide strategic insights to the organization. Conversely, a poorly designed structure can lead to inefficiencies, confusion, and a lack of strategic alignment.

6. **What Role Does Technology Play in the Structure of the HR Function?**

Technology plays a pivotal role in the structure of the HR function. HR technologies can automate routine tasks, freeing up HR professionals to focus on strategic activities. They can also facilitate communication and collaboration within the HR team and across the organization, impacting how HR roles are structured and coordinated.

7. **How Should the HR Function Be Structured to Support Strategic HRM?**

To support strategic HRM, the HR function should be structured in a way that allows HR professionals to work closely with other business units. This may involve the business partner model or a matrix structure. The HR team should also have roles focused on strategic activities such as workforce planning, talent management, and organizational development.

8. **How Can the HR Function Evolve as the Organization Grows?**

As the organization grows, the HR function often needs to become more specialized and sophisticated. This may involve creating new roles, implementing HR technologies, or restructuring the HR department. It's important for HR leaders to anticipate these changes and plan for them proactively to support organizational growth.

9. **What Challenges Can Arise from the Structure of the HR Function?**

Challenges that can arise from the structure of the HR function include:

- Role confusion or duplication of efforts.

- Communication breakdowns or silos.

- Difficulty adapting to changes in the organization or business environment.

These challenges can be addressed by regularly reviewing and adjusting the HR structure, providing clear communication about roles and responsibilities, and fostering a flexible and collaborative culture in the HR team.

10. **How Can an Organization Determine the Best Structure for Its HR Function?**

Determining the best structure for the HR function involves understanding the organization's strategic objectives, assessing the current HR structure, identifying gaps or inefficiencies, and then designing a new structure that better fits the organization's needs. This process should involve input from HR team members, other key stakeholders, and potentially external experts.

Employee and Labor Relations

Understanding Employee Rights and Privacy

HR professionals carry immense responsibility to uphold legal and ethical standards protecting employees. Beyond compliance, a strong rights foundation enables trust, engagement and productivity. This chapter provides an overview of key employee rights, privacy laws, and HR safeguarding imperatives.

Honoring Protected Classes

Understand protections against discrimination, harassment or unfair treatment based on characteristics like race, gender, age, religion, disability etc. Ensure equal access and prevent discriminatory actions.

Enforcing Safety Rights

Provide required safety training, protective equipment, OSHA reporting and accommodations for injured/pregnant workers. Familiarize all with emergency procedures and rights to report issues.

Allowing Speech and Representation

With exceptions, employees retain rights to free speech, voicing opinions and participating in protected organizing activities under NLRB laws. Do not infringe without cause.

Permitting Reasonable Accommodation

Make good faith efforts to reasonably accommodate disabilities and religious practices per ADA and EEOC regulations unless causing undue hardship. Engage in interactive dialogue.

Maintaining Confidentiality

Never disclose private employee information (health, performance, status) without a clear business need. Limit access. Obtain consent where appropriate.

Separating Sensitive Data

Keep sensitive records like medical forms and payroll locked with restricted access. Never use for purposes beyond initial need.

Providing Transparency

Inform employees of rights clearly during onboarding and in handbooks. Explain legal exceptions transparently rather than seeming heavy-handed.

Establishing Compliance Policies

Document detailed policies addressing standards, procedures and accountability mechanisms that uphold rights and prevent infringements.

Training Managers

Educate managers extensively on protecting rights, avoiding inherent bias, maintaining confidentiality, properly reporting issues and enforcement protocols.

Auditing and Correcting

Routinely audit policies, programs and systems for potential rights violations. Analyze complaints and incidents to prevent recurrence. Act swiftly if issues occur.

Upholding employee rights and privacy builds engagement and trust. With knowledge, vigilance and compassion, HR enables a fair, lawful and ethical people centered environment. We set the tone.

Managing Employee Disciplinary Procedures

In any organization, maintaining a harmonious and productive work environment is crucial. Occasionally, situations may arise where an employee's behavior or performance falls short of the organization's expectations. In such cases, a well-defined and fair disciplinary procedure becomes essential. It not only helps organizations handle such incidents effectively, but it also protects the rights of employees, fostering a sense of justice and equity.

Understanding Employee Disciplinary Procedures

Employee disciplinary procedures are formal processes that an organization uses to address an employee's unsatisfactory behavior or performance. These procedures can tackle a range of issues, from minor misconduct, such as persistent lateness, to more grave offenses like harassment or fraud.

Importance of Disciplinary Procedures

Having a clear and fair disciplinary procedure is beneficial for several reasons:

- **Clarity and Consistency:** It provides a clear framework for handling disciplinary issues, ensuring consistency across the organization.

- **Legal Protection:** It helps protect the organization and its employees from legal repercussions by ensuring that disciplinary actions are carried out fairly and lawfully.

- **Conflict Resolution:** It offers a structured way to address and resolve workplace conflicts, thereby maintaining harmony and productivity.

- **Performance Improvement:** It serves as a tool for managing poor performance and encouraging improvement.

Key Elements of Disciplinary Procedures

A comprehensive disciplinary procedure typically includes the following elements:

1. **Written Policy:** The disciplinary procedure should be clearly documented in a written policy that is accessible to all employees. The policy should outline the process, possible disciplinary actions, and the employee's rights during the process.

2. **Investigation:** Before any disciplinary action, an impartial investigation should be conducted to gather relevant facts and evidence.

3. **Notification:** The employee should be informed about the concerns regarding their behavior or performance, supported by evidence where necessary.

4. **Hearing:** The employee should be given the opportunity to present their case at a formal hearing or meeting. They should also have the right to be accompanied by a colleague or union representative.

5. **Decision:** After the hearing, a decision should be made based on the evidence and arguments presented. The employee should be informed of this decision in writing.

6. **Appeal:** The employee should have the right to appeal the decision if they believe it is unfair. The appeal should be heard by a manager who was not involved in the original decision.

Implementing Disciplinary Procedures

When it comes to implementing disciplinary procedures, here are some best practices:

- **Fairness:** Ensure the procedure is carried out fairly and impartially. Avoid any form of discrimination or bias.

- **Confidentiality:** Keep the details of the disciplinary procedure confidential to respect the privacy of all parties involved.

- **Documentation:** Document every step of the procedure, including meetings, decisions, and actions taken. This can serve as a reference in case of any dispute or legal action.

- **Consistency:** Apply the procedure consistently for all employees, regardless of their role or status in the organization.

- **Communication:** Keep the lines of communication open with the employee throughout the process. Ensure they understand the procedure and their rights.

The Role of HR in Disciplinary Procedures

The Human Resources (HR) department plays a crucial role in managing disciplinary procedures. They are responsible for developing the disciplinary policy, advising managers on its application, and ensuring it is implemented fairly and consistently. HR also helps handle investigations, hearings, and appeals, and maintains records of the process.

In the complex world of work, disciplinary issues can be challenging to navigate. However, with a clear, fair, and consistent procedure, organizations can manage these issues effectively, protecting both the organization's interests and the rights of employees.

Workplace Safety and Health

Promoting a safe and healthy work environment is not merely a legal obligation but a strategic imperative for organizations. A robust approach to workplace safety and health not only minimizes the risk of accidents and illness but also enhances employee satisfaction, productivity, and the overall reputation of the company.

Understanding Workplace Safety and Health

Workplace safety and health encompasses a broad range of practices and policies designed to protect employees from hazards that may cause injury or illness. These hazards can come in various forms, including physical, chemical, biological, ergonomic, or psychosocial. The goal is to prevent accidents and health issues, thereby ensuring a productive and congenial work environment.

The Importance of Workplace Safety and Health

A strong focus on workplace safety and health has several benefits for organizations:

- **Employee Well-being:** It protects employees from injuries and illnesses, thereby promoting their overall well-being.

- **Productivity:** It reduces downtime due to accidents or illnesses, thereby enhancing productivity.

- **Compliance:** It ensures compliance with laws and regulations related to workplace safety and health.

- **Reputation:** It enhances the organization's reputation as a safe and healthy place to work.

- **Cost Savings:** It reduces costs associated with accidents, such as medical expenses, compensation, and lost productivity.

Developing a Workplace Safety and Health Program

Creating a comprehensive workplace safety and health program involves several key steps:

1. **Risk Assessment:** Identify potential hazards in the workplace and assess the risk they pose to employees.

2. **Policies and Procedures:** Develop clear policies and procedures to manage identified risks. This could include safety guidelines, emergency procedures, and health protocols.

3. **Training:** Provide regular training to employees on safety practices and health policies. Ensure they understand the potential hazards and how to avoid them.

4. **Communication:** Maintain open lines of communication about safety and health matters. Encourage employees to report potential hazards or safety concerns.

5. **Monitoring and Evaluation:** Regularly monitor and evaluate the effectiveness of your safety and health program. This might involve safety audits, health surveys, or accident analysis.

Role of Managers in Promoting Workplace Safety and Health

Managers play a critical role in promoting workplace safety and health. They are responsible for implementing safety and health policies, ensuring compliance, and fostering a culture of safety. Managers should lead by example, demonstrating safe behavior, and responding promptly and effectively to safety and health concerns.

Legal Aspects of Workplace Safety and Health

Workplace safety and health is governed by various laws and regulations, which vary by country and industry. Failure to comply with these laws can result in penalties, legal action, or even closure of the business. Therefore, organizations should stay updated on relevant laws and ensure full compliance.

In the increasingly competitive business environment, organizations cannot afford to ignore workplace safety and health. It's not just about preventing accidents and illnesses—it's about creating a work environment where employees feel safe, valued, and cared for. This, in turn, can boost employee engagement, productivity, and loyalty, thereby enhancing the organization's overall performance.

While the physical safety of employees is critical, organizations should also pay attention to their mental and emotional health. Work-related stress, burnout, and mental health issues are becoming increasingly prevalent, and they can have a significant impact on employee well-being and productivity. Therefore, a comprehensive approach to workplace safety and health should include strategies to promote mental and emotional well-being, such as stress management programs, flexible work arrangements, and mental health support.

Practice Questions and Detailed Answers

Employee and labor relations encompass the multifaceted relationships between an organization and its employees, including individual employees, groups of employees, and employee organizations like labor unions. This chapter will delve into ten practice questions and provide comprehensive answers that will help you better understand employee and labor relations.
   1. **What are Employee and Labor Relations?**
Employee and labor relations refer to the management of relationships between an organization and its employees. This includes addressing employee concerns and grievances, managing conflict, ensuring fair treatment, and negotiating collective agreements with labor unions. The goal is to foster a positive, productive, and harmonious workplace.
   2. **Why are Employee and Labor Relations Important?**
Employee and labor relations are crucial because:

- They contribute to a positive organizational culture.
- They can affect employee morale, engagement, and productivity.
- They assist in preventing and resolving workplace conflicts.
- They ensure compliance with labor laws and collective agreements.

3. What is the Role of HR in Employee and Labor Relations?

The role of HR in employee and labor relations includes:
- Advising management on employee relations strategies and policies.
- Addressing employee concerns and grievances.
- Facilitating communication between management and employees.
- Negotiating and administering collective agreements with labor unions.
- Ensuring compliance with labor laws.

4. What is a Labor Union?

A labor union is an organization of workers who come together to negotiate with employers about terms and conditions of employment, such as wages, work hours, and workplace safety. Unions provide a collective voice for employees and aim to ensure fair treatment.

5. How Do Labor Unions Affect Employee and Labor Relations?

Labor unions can significantly affect employee and labor relations. They can influence terms and conditions of employment through collective bargaining, provide representation for employees in grievance procedures, and encourage a more equitable balance of power between employers and employees. However, they can also lead to conflicts and disruptions if employer-union relations are not managed well.

6. What is Collective Bargaining?

Collective bargaining is the process in which labor unions negotiate with employers on behalf of their members to establish collective agreements. The negotiations cover various employment issues, including wages, benefits, working conditions, and dispute resolution procedures.

7. How Can Conflicts in the Workplace Be Managed?

Conflicts in the workplace can be managed through:
- Clear communication: Addressing issues openly and honestly can often prevent misunderstandings from escalating into conflicts.
- Mediation: A neutral third party can facilitate a resolution.
- Grievance procedures: These provide a formal process for employees to raise concerns.
- Training: Conflict resolution training can equip employees and managers with the skills to handle disputes effectively.

8. What are the Legal Aspects of Employee and Labor Relations?

The legal aspects of employee and labor relations include laws and regulations that govern employment relationships, such as:

- Labor laws: These regulate the relationship between employers and unions.
- Employment laws: These cover issues like discrimination, harassment, and workplace safety.
- Collective agreements: These are legally binding contracts negotiated with labor unions.

HR must ensure that the organization complies with these legal requirements to avoid legal risks and maintain a fair and respectful workplace.

9. **How Can an Organization Foster Positive Employee Relations?**

An organization can foster positive employee relations by:
- Communicating openly and honestly with employees.
- Treating employees fairly and respectfully.
- Providing opportunities for employee feedback and involvement.
- Recognizing and rewarding employee contributions.
- Addressing employee concerns promptly and effectively.

10. **What Challenges Can Arise in Employee and Labor Relations?**

Challenges in employee and labor relations can include:
- Conflicts between employees or between employees and management.
- Negotiating and implementing collective agreements.
- Dealing with grievances and disciplinary issues.
- Navigating changes in labor laws or workplace demographics.
- Balancing the interests of employees, the organization, and other stakeholders.

Embracing positive employee and labor relations is much more than a legal or contractual obligation. It forms the cornerstone of an engaging and inclusive workplace culture, promoting harmony, productivity, and mutual respect. As the business landscape evolves, so do the dynamics of employee and labor relations. This necessitates a proactive and empathetic HR approach, constantly aligning with the changing needs and aspirations of the workforce.

BONUS Course

Made in the USA
Las Vegas, NV
30 October 2023

79964451R00059